OUR CANADA

OUR CANADA

Edited by Leo Heaps

James Lorimer & Company, Publishers
Toronto 1991

Canadian Cataloguing in Publication Data

Main entry under title:

Our Canada
ISBN 1-55028-355-3 (bound) ISBN 1-55028-353-7 (pbk.)

1. Co-operative Commonwealth Federation - History.
2. New Democratic Party - History.   I. Heaps, Leo, 1923-

JL197.C608 1991   324.27107   C91-094854-2

Cover photo: Photo Feature Ltd.

James Lorimer & Company, Publishers
Egerton Ryerson Memorial Building
35 Britain Street
Toronto, Ontario
M5A 1R7

Printed and bound in Canada

Contents

Preface

This book has been written to satisfy a growing hunger for knowledge among those many thousands who are unacquainted with the origins of the New Democratic Party. This includes most Canadians. From the beginning, almost a century ago, the ideal of social justice was the goal of the small band of men and women who dedicated themselves to the long struggle to reform the existing social order. What the pioneers lacked in numbers they made up for in purpose and dedication. Dreamers who envisaged a society founded on the truest of democratic principles, they felt at times that they were reaching for the stars.

The pioneers took us from the edge of darkness towards the light of new social ideals. They dared when others stood back and hesitated. They risked their personal liberty and the censure of society at a time when to be a radical and advocate change was to be branded a Bolshevik or a communist. We have come as far as we have because of the courage and perseverance of these men and women.

Many of these pioneers who first settled the West were schooled in the tradition of British working-class institutions. They were largely poor or middle class in origin, church ministers and tradespeople, labour council members and academics, union members and small businesspeople who lived at a time when exploitation of the working population was commonplace. But these pioneers had one quality in common. They wanted all Canadians, regardless of their background, to have an equal chance in life, to enjoy a living wage and peace of mind. They were considered heretics — but they maintained their course, despite the cost. However, none of them advocated revolution. Some were pacifists through religious conviction; all were men and women of peace. J. S. Woodsworth, the first leader of the federal party, was a church minister and pacifist. A. A. Heaps, by trade an upholsterer, was also a pacifist during the First World War. M. J. Coldwell was a school principal, Tommy Douglas a minister of the church, David Lewis a lawyer, Agnes Macphail, the first woman member of Parliament, a teacher, and Angus MacInnis a streetcar conductor, while Grace MacInnis was an educator and Stanley Knowles a minister and typesetter. And so the list went.

The names of these and many other exceptional individuals who were among the founders of this movement are fading slowly from memory. We hope this book will bring them back to life. Some never held public office but nonetheless played vital roles. Men like Frank Scott, Dean of Law at McGill, poet, defender of individual rights, was one of the first presidents of the Co-operative Commonwealth Federation and a rare individual. His contributions and influence were quite considerable. Frank Underhill, another contemporary, made an outstanding contribution. There were members of Parliament like Clarence Gillis and Alistair Stewart. These are only a few who deserve special mention. The fragility of human memory is both unforgivable and understandable. But somehow, somewhere, most of the people who fought the hard struggle will be commemorated in the pages that follow. They all believed in one nation, one united Canada. They were patriots, these patient men and women. They never gave up. They waited, knowing that the battle might be long but that they would succeed in the creation of a more just and humane society.

Acknowledgements

I wish to thank the Douglas-Coldwell Foundation for their assistance in the production of *Our Canada*, and in particular director Kalman Kaplansky. The encouragement of Dick Proctor and his understanding of the purpose of this book made it possible. Stephen Lewis also deserves my warmest appreciation.

Part I
The Pioneers

A Note on the Biographies

These biographical profiles have been done, for the most part, of those parliamentarians who attended the first Co-operative Commonwealth Federation caucus in the House of Commons in Ottawa in 1935, and consequently made history. There are, however, a few exceptions. One is the inclusion of David Lewis, who was with the party from the early days and later became its leader. The other exceptions are Grace MacInnis, Stanley Knowles and Agnes Macphail, whose place will be unquestioned. The inclusion here of these biographies does not mean that there were not other pioneers whose zeal and dedication made them major contributors to social democracy in Canada. Simply, the line had to be drawn at a certain point. Grant MacNeil is excluded for lack of sufficient information. But he was a man of exceptional ability. And as a member of Parliament, he too sat in that historic caucus meeting. We ask forgiveness on behalf of all those men and women, past and present, who do not appear in these pages. As one of the contributors to this volume said when he was asked to compile an honour roll, he had to give up after several dozen names, because there were still so many more to add.

James Shaver Woodsworth

Leo Heaps

James Shaver Woodsworth was born in 1874 and died in 1942, yet his influence is still deeply felt in the heart and soul of the New Democratic Party and, indeed, in our nation itself. This saintly looking figure with his small goatee, his clear blue eyes and fragile physique possessed a strength of character that belied his looks. There are many who believe Woodsworth will always rank among the great political figures of Canada. True, he had his bitter opponents, his weaknesses and his differences with those close to him, and he was disliked by members of the established interests, but no one who really knew him well could hate J. S. Woodsworth. His motives were too clear, and his honesty in all things large and small always unquestioned. To the last, he maintained his ideals of pacifism at a time when the world was changing about him and when he stood alone even in the councils of his own party.

J. S. Woodsworth was born into comfortable middle-class circumstances on an Ontario farm. His parents and grandparents were staunch Methodists, loyal to the traditions of the British Empire and confirmed conservatives. His father preached to churches in Northern Ontario until the family moved to Manitoba where he was ordained as a church pastor. J. S. Woodsworth, the eldest child of six, followed in his father's footsteps after a

brilliant academic career at Wesley College in Winnipeg.
In 1900, Woodsworth became a Methodist preacher and
it looked as if he was settling down to a career of
middle-class respectability surrounded by all the com-
forts of an existence that his father before him had
enjoyed. But unexpected emotions were stirring in the
heart of the young minister. In 1899, Woodsworth decided to attend Oxford for a year. His travels to Edin-
burgh and London and his visit to the settlement houses
in the slums of those cities left a lasting impression. He
would remember for the remainder of his life these
scenes of humiliating poverty and degradation of the
human spirit. When he returned to his well-to-do congregation in Winnipeg, his life no longer seemed to have
anything in common with the abject misery he had
witnessed in Europe or that existed in the slums of
Winnipeg or among the growing army of unemployed
that roamed the nation searching for work. These
people should be his congregation. The radical nature of
Woodsworth's sermons soon drew the ire and dissatis-
faction of his respectable parishioners and it was not
long before they forced his dismissal.

Woodsworth had now consciously chosen the path he
was to follow for the rest of his life. At twenty-seven, he
knew what he wanted to do. Something was wrong with
a system that could breed such comfort in his parish and
at the same time permit the chronic poverty that surrounded him on all sides. Woodsworth quit the ministry.
But he was determined he would not stop preaching. His
congregation, however, would change and become that
other world he had seen and whose misery had continued
to disturb him. Indeed, it possessed him. He would
remain forever in his pulpit; but the message he would
deliver would not be the same.

In 1916, Woodsworth held a government job as director of the Bureau of Social Research. This was during the First World War. As a conscientious objector, he refused to register for service as a soldier and was fired from his government position. He headed west to Vancouver where he worked for a while as a longshoreman, making barely enough to supply food for his wife and young family. All the while, he spoke to the longshoremen on the evils of the present society where there was dire want amidst great wealth. He taught and educated the longshoremen, as he had done with the slum dwellers and railway employees of Winnipeg. Although always frail of physique, he possessed formidable energy and was obsessed by the single-mindedness of his mission. His wife, Lucy, educated and also from a well-to-do family, had long since resigned herself to the task her husband had undertaken and the personal sacrifices she would have to make. It was as if Woodsworth had become in the twentieth century one of the Disciples himself, prepared when necessary to partake of any job or whatever meagre fare was available in order to deliver his message. Woodsworth wrote continuously—pamphlets, articles in the *Western Labour News* and in any journals that would print his essays. He preached his sermons of socialism with inexhaustible zeal in labour halls, homes and on street corners to the unemployed.

When he arrived back in Winnipeg in 1919, three weeks after the Winnipeg General Strike had engulfed the city in a cataclysm of civil warfare, he immediately allied himself with the workers' cause. Although Woodsworth was not one of the strike leaders, he quickly threw himself into the struggle which had provoked this massive protest of the unions and paralysed the city. He assumed the role of editor of the *Western Labour News* when his friend, William Ivens, was arrested on the

charge of seditious conspiracy. Later Woodsworth
would be arrested himself for printing, among other
things, passages from the Book of Isaiah. He and Fred
Dixon were both accused of seditious libel, fortunately
a less serious charge than the accusation of seditious
conspiracy directed against John Queen, William Ivens,
A. A. Heaps and others. Later the charges against Woodsworth were dropped.

In 1921 Woodsworth joined the Winnipeg Independent Labour Party and became their candidate in the
federal election of December of that year. In spite of the
total opposition of the press and business, he was elected
with a majority of 3700 votes. The first socialist to enter
the Canadian House of Commons took his seat in 1922.
Woodsworth had at last the forum from where he would
launch his views to the widest possible audience. He
linked up with William Irvine from Calgary and the
Progressives, a farmers' party that effectively held the
balance of power in Ottawa. There were plenty of injustices in the nation for Woodsworth to complain about.
He saw them on every side. The miners of Cape Breton
were being forced into a strike for living wages and
Woodsworth witnessed first-hand the tragic poverty in
which they lived. He spoke out eloquently for them in
the Commons, but to deaf ears. In Nova Scotia the
steelworkers also sought a living wage but their strike
was crushed by the militia and the police, their leaders
jailed for sedition. Miners were working a fourteen-hour
day six days a week for twelve dollars. Judges were
discovered to be directors of the coal mines and steel
plants while ministers of the Crown were revealed as
shareholders of the companies that they were exploiting.
It was an age when voices against the power of the
establishment were few. Woodsworth, as the sole labour
member of Parliament, spoke alone. Sometimes he was

joined by William Irvine and Agnes Macphail, who was one of the Progressives. Woodsworth believed he was preaching a moral doctrine against a system that could not look after its people and, moreover, did not seem to care.

The most successful labour party in Canada was the Winnipeg Independent Labour Party. Three years after Woodsworth entered Parliament, A. A. Heaps joined him in Ottawa, elected in Winnipeg North as a labour member. Heaps's presence in the Commons as labour's second socialist member gave Woodsworth much-needed support. Their association would last fifteen years. Together they would have a chance to remake history. During this period, Woodsworth carefully chronicled police brutality, the invasion of homes by the constabulary, deportations without trial, censorship of the press. He was personally repulsed by a society that had spawned a race of bailiffs who callously repossessed the meagre possessions of the unemployed. Woodsworth was the conscience of the people and was to become, eventually, the moral conscience of the present party.

In 1933 the Co-operative Commonwealth Federation replaced the Independent Labour Party, over the bitter protests of the Winnipeg organization. John Queen, mayor of Winnipeg, member of the Manitoba Legislature and one of the strike leaders in the Winnipeg General Strike, never accepted the new organization. A. A. Heaps, who out of deference to Woodsworth won re-election under the CCF label, was only lukewarm to the idea, as were many of his comrades. These were turbulent days. However, on the federal level, by 1939 Woodsworth led seven CCF members. And they could always count on the support of Agnes Macphail until she was defeated in 1944. Meanwhile, amidst the clouds of war, Woodsworth, a pacifist to the last, carried on his campaign of speeches and writings throughout the nation. His energy undiminished, he travelled to Europe and in 1937 to Russia, where he was shaken by the abuses that he witnessed within its totalitarian regime. The Russian Revolution had fired the imagination of the liberal-minded, but no one dreamed of the brutality that would follow. The first seeds of doubt about the effectiveness of economic reform without freedom were sown in Woodsworth's mind. Freedom from want without freedom from fear was not worth the price.

Until 1939, Woodsworth campaigned with undiminished vigour for the right of workers to strike and form unions without risking the penalty of dismissal by employers. Meanwhile, other forces were rising in the world too powerful for one man to halt. Woodsworth held onto his religious ideal of pacifism even in the face of the Second World War, and never accepted the idea that even the most devoted man of peace must on occasion march to save his freedom.

In the summer of 1939, the CCF National Council defeated Woodsworth's motion of non-participation in the war. There were voices in the council who protested that this was not an imperialist war, as Woodsworth claimed, but one of survival against a brutal dictatorship. Perhaps if there had been enough years left, Woodsworth might have re-examined the basis of his life's teaching. But fate intervened. In the following year leadership passed from his hands to those of M. J. Coldwell. Woodsworth suffered a debilitating stroke and died in 1942.

In the House of Commons, Mackenzie King, the prime minister of Canada, paid his tribute to his friend Woodsworth. "There are few men in this Parliament for whom in some particulars, I have greater respect than the Leader of the Co-operative Commonwealth Federation. I admire him in my heart because time and again he has had the courage to say what lay on his conscience regardless of what the world might think of him. A man of that calibre is an ornament to any Parliament."

Few leaders of any political movement could achieve the purity of motive or make the many personal sacrifices that characterized J. S. Woodsworth's existence. The greatest gift James Shaver Woodsworth gave to the nation and the New Democratic Party was the selfless example of his life.

Abraham Albert Heaps

Leo Heaps

A. A. Heaps was in almost all ways the opposite of J. S. Woodsworth. It has often been said that if Woodsworth was the leader, then Heaps was the party. Abraham Heaps was born in 1889 amidst grim poverty in the immigrant section of Leeds. Here poor Jews made their home when they came to England from Europe, late in the last century. At the age of twelve he was forced to leave school to support his family, although he had distinguished himself by winning several scholarships. He set forth into the grimy, soot-infested industrial factory district of Leeds to become an upholsterer's apprentice. Like Woodsworth, Heaps was then a pacifist and through his own reading had become a devoted socialist. He believed that the social and economic system he saw about him was not designed for the benefit of the people.

In 1912, he immigrated to Winnipeg and punched in as an upholsterer in the old workshop of the Canadian Pacific Railway. Later, when his wife arrived, he moved into the immigrant North End of the city, which became Abe Heaps's crucible where he forged new friendships and ideas in the heated debates that took place in the labour temples. What Heaps lacked in education, he made up for with a natural sharpness of mind, an amazing memory for details, a brilliant, analytical brain and a wit that could turn aside the barbs of his political foes. His associates were men and women who would play a major role in transforming the political character of Manitoba and the nation.

Heaps knew exactly what he wanted to do with his life. Unlike Woodsworth, he was not the implacable foe of capitalism. He believed that a man had the right to own property, but what he wanted was to replace the brutality and savage grip of capitalist society with a better system that did not exploit the worker. Sweatshops and child labour were common in Canada. Heaps sought a humanitarian style of government that would disavow unemployment as a tool to discipline the workforce.

In 1917 Abe Heaps was elected to the Winnipeg Trades and Labour Council in a city that had become bitterly divided. A deepening cleavage between established interests and labour was growing without anyone being able to control it. The antagonism was further fuelled by the government policies of conscription and registration. The First World War was viewed by most socialists as an imperialist struggle for markets that had little to do with the common man, either in Germany or Canada.

In 1918 Heaps stood for alderman as a labour candidate. At his defeat he suspected fraud. A judicial inquiry substantiated his claim of corruption and the election was declared invalid. In the new election Abe Heaps won handily and took his seat along with his good friend, John Queen, on the Winnipeg City Council. These two men became the spokesmen of labour during this period of growing union militancy and deep unrest that threatened to disrupt the life of the city. The stage was being set for the dramatic and momentous events of the Winnipeg General Strike, which was to follow shortly.

In the springtime of 1919 a general strike paralysed Winnipeg. When the police and fire departments joined the workers, the army and the Royal Canadian Mounted Police took over. At 2:00 a.m. one summer morning in June of 1919, the young Heaps was arrested at his home on the charge of seditious conspiracy, handcuffed, driven to Stony Mountain Penitentiary and thrown into a cell as a common criminal. He was told he was to be deported in a few days as an undesirable alien, although he had been born in England. However, a massive protest by labour at the arrest of the strike leaders made the Borden government in Ottawa reconsider. In a few days Heaps was out on bail. For over a year he travelled the country raising money for his trial and those of his colleagues. For twelve months, Heaps and his wife were forced to live from hand to mouth until finally the day of the trial arrived. As a defendant, he had prepared ninety-two pages of handwritten notes that would be the basis of his defence. The trial of Heaps and his colleagues lasted almost six months. As his own counsel, Heaps summed up his case to the jury for eight hours. Alone of all the first six defendants, he was acquitted. His colleagues went to jail, sentenced to two years or more. When Abe Heaps walked out of the courtroom a free man, he said, "I would have rather gone to jail with the others."

In 1926 Heaps was elected member of Parliament for Winnipeg North and joined J. S. Woodsworth as the second member of the Independent Labour Party. As fate would have it, Woodsworth and Heaps in 1926 were in a powerful position. They held the balance of power. From his first day, the new member began his long fight for the introduction of old age pensions and unemployment insurance, which he eventually would be instrumental in making law. Heaps drew up a draft of a bill and showed it to Woodsworth, and they presented it to Mackenzie King at a private meeting. In turn, the Prime Minister sent a letter to the two members promising to introduce the legislation on unemployment insurance and old age pensions as well as amend the Immigration Act and the Criminal Code as it related to deportation without trial. The Prime Minister then offered the position of Minister of Labour first to Woodsworth and then to Heaps. Both men refused in turn. They could not be bought. Mackenzie King kept his word and introduced the old age pension bill in the 1926 session, but procedural wrangling with the old phantom of provincial rights kept it from becoming law.

The next fifteen years were to establish Heaps as an exceptional debater. He knew from memory almost every clause of the British Unemployment Insurance and Old Age Pensions Acts. He had read and continued to read voluminously. Woodsworth, by both background and education, was on equal footing with any parliamentarian, but Heaps could not forget his meagre education or that he grew up in poverty in the slums of Leeds. Wilfred Eggelston of the parliamentary press gallery summed up the difference between Woodsworth and Heaps: "Woodsworth is a humanitarian. Heaps is an advanced liberal and realist." But these two men always had respect and friendship for one another.

In 1926 the Winnipeg General Strike was debated in Parliament. Heaps finally had the forum he had been waiting for. It was ideas the government feared, he said. Ideas of equality of labour, a living wage, security, ideas that could create more employment and break the yoke that bound the worker. Parliament listened to Heaps respectfully. Sometimes he was a voice only supported by his colleagues, J. S. Woodsworth and Agnes Macphail. But something else had happened in Parliament that he had not anticipated. W. L. Mackenzie King, that strange mystic, and R. B. Bennett, the leader of the Conservatives—a deeply religious man and a millionaire at a time when there were few millionaires in Canada—had befriended this socialist whose political views were heresy to most members of their parties.

Meanwhile, bread lines grew throughout the nation as the Great Depression struck, reaping a sad and devastating harvest among Canadians. The bailiffs stalked the land. It was a difficult time for Heaps to face the workers of Canada under a system that had failed them in a land of plenty. R. B. Bennett, now the Conservative prime minister (he was elected in 1931), would often meet privately with Heaps, through whom he felt he had a direct contact with working men and women. The Prime Minister admitted during these conversations that the system that had made him a millionaire had failed the people if it could produce a catastrophe like the Great Depression.

On April 29, 1931, Bennett gave to A. A. Heaps one of his rare moments in Parliament. On that date Heaps introduced again his motion for a system of insurance against unemployment, sickness and invalidity. The motion was seconded by J. S. Woodsworth. R. B. Bennett then rose in his seat as Prime Minister to accept the resolution. Speaker after speaker came to their feet to endorse the proposal. It was a triumph for Heaps. Several months after this event, Bennett wrote Heaps a letter to ask if he would accept a Senate appointment. The offer was magnanimous. Abe Heaps would be Canada's first labour senator and first Jewish member of the Upper House. But his answer was no. He believed in the abolition of the Senate and wanted instead an elected second chamber. He thanked Bennett, but his duty lay in the improvement of the lot of the people to whom he had devoted his life.

In the mid-thirties the Nazis came to power in Germany, and Heaps and the small contingent of CCF members tried to pry open the closed doors of Canada for the victims of Nazi persecution. But they met too much opposition from the government. In 1939, as the German jackboots were trampling across Europe, Heaps made one of his most stirring pleas to save the refugees, but his eloquence fell on deaf ears. Somehow, Abe Heaps felt he had not much time left in Parliament. He introduced a motion to reduce the age of eligibility for old age pensions from seventy to sixty-five. Heaps, the Prime Minister said, was never satisfied. But his world was changing. Woodsworth would soon suffer a paralysing stroke. M. J. Coldwell was now the unofficial leader of the CCF. Abe Heaps's wife had died after a long, painful illness. In his last days in Parliament, Heaps made a number of moving pleas for peace. He had always been a confirmed pacifist, but now the world was different. In and out of the small CCF caucus Heaps led the fight to change the pacifist sentiment to meet the reality of fascism that threatened the civilized world. Only England stood in its way.

In the 1940 election, the Communists ran a strong candidate against Heaps in Winnipeg North, as they always did. The Liberal nominee reminded this immigrant constituency that Heaps had once been a pacifist. By a narrow margin Abe Heaps went down to defeat and the working men and women of Canada lost one of their champions. Later that same year a phone call came to the boarding house where Heaps lived with his young son in Ottawa. Prime Minister Mackenzie King was on the phone. He asked if Abe Heaps would consider joining the government as Minister of Labour. Three times in his career, an opportunity seldom offered to a Canadian socialist presented itself. Twice he had been offered the portfolio of labour and once a seat in the Senate. Abe Heaps could not accept in good conscience, although he had little money and, at the time, no prospects. Later he became the grain controller at the Lakehead and then Unemployment Insurance Commissioner. His old friend, David Lewis, tried to convince him to run for Parliament again, but Heaps seemed no longer interested.

In the spring of 1954 Abe Heaps visited England in frail health. There he was stricken with a fatal heart attack and died alone. His two sons arrived too late to be by his bedside. He was buried in Leeds, the town where he was born, in a small cemetery often shrouded by the thick grey smoke that drifts in from the factories of this working people's city. In one of those factories Abe Heaps had worked as a boy upholsterer for thirty shillings a week.

M. J. Coldwell

David Heaps

On February 13, 1936, M. J. Coldwell, the newly elected Co-operative Commonwealth Federation member of Parliament for Rosetown-Biggar, in Saskatchewan, made his first speech in the House of Commons — a probing analysis of Depression-era problems in the nation's agricultural heartland. A veteran member of the chamber then rose to observe: "I have been in public life for many years, and I have never listened to a maiden speech with greater interest than I did to the honourable gentleman who has just taken his seat. I predict this young man will go far in the public life of this country."

Then forty-seven years of age, the British-born Coldwell already had compiled a lustrous record of attainment in his adopted province of Saskatchewan. Those who knew him there would not have been surprised at the acclaim evoked by his address.

In the years 1945 to 1947, M. J. Coldwell, as the CCF parliamentary leader, had a small personal staff comprising a parliamentary secretary and two secretary-typists. They all felt that they had had good fortune to be associated with a man whose private values matched his public professions. M. J., as he was called by all who knew him, was a model of patience and consideration to everyone who worked for him, including one aide whose prior military background was a less-than-ideal preparation for the new tasks he was to encounter. Among those who knew him then, basic impressions have not dimmed, even with the passage of more than four decades. On the contrary, they now view Coldwell's human qualities, moral courage and public contributions within a larger historical perspective, and they loom today more impressively than ever. In retrospect, this remarkable human being, for whom public service was the highest and most noble calling, can be seen as the primary architect in transforming a regional reformist party into a true alternative to the established two-party system.

M. J.'s parliamentary colleagues at the time — Angus MacInnis, Stanley Knowles, Clarence Gillis, Alistair Stewart and others—formed an outstanding team committed to social and economic justice. Yet even among this sterling assembly, Coldwell's rare combination of total integrity, innate modesty and intellectual probity shone like a beacon light. His exemplary public personality was the mirror image of the truly virtuous inner man. Even during periods of extreme stress, Coldwell was unvaryingly courteous and considerate, incapable of pettiness or unkindness in thought or deed. Unlike some prominent party intellectuals of the day, he was never doctrinaire, self-righteous or self-important. Professor Dean McHenry of the University of California, an authority on British Commonwealth political parties, described Coldwell as a "moderate socialist and internationalist with an unusual brilliance, attractive personality, and great devotion and vision." It was only logical that the parliamentary press corps, shrewd observers of the Ottawa scene, should have viewed M. J. Coldwell as the nation's outstanding legislator.

An Ontario newspaper lauded Coldwell early in his national career for his "oratory, intelligence and unparalleled ability on the public platforms," but noted also, "we sometimes get the impression that Mr. Coldwell revels more in kindly sentiments than bitter denunciation, although he can hit hard when he desires to castigate the Tories and Liberals." Like others who did not know Coldwell, the editor mistook external politeness for a possible lack of internal intensity. Underneath a cloak of natural courtesy, M. J.'s convictions were crystal clear and his principles unflinchingly steadfast. Civility and mutual respect were to him the essence of personal and professional relationships.

Coldwell, although he was a public figure in constant demand, was always a devoted husband and caring father. He never hinted during busy workdays at his onerous nightly vigils. Aided by his devoted daughter, Margaret, a nurse, he coped daily with the crippling illness of his beloved and by then bed-ridden wife and companion, Norah. Some mornings he arrived at the office later than usual, his face blanched by fatigue, and his staff knew that there had been an unusually bad night. Offers to relieve him so that he could be rested for the morning were courteously but firmly declined; he explained that a newcomer to the house could not anticipate Mrs. Coldwell's nocturnal needs and would not know how to carry her when required. It was quickly apparent that he would not accept outside help for what he viewed as a family responsibility.

Coldwell's early background may provide insights into the man he became. Born in 1888 of modest circumstances amid the settled Victorian values of rural southern England, he was baptized Major (a maternal family surname) James William. Winning a rare teacher-training scholarship to University College, Exeter, Coldwell was an excellent all-round student. In his final year he became engaged to Norah Dunsford, a fellow student whose father, a country editor and publisher, had visited

Canada and expressed enthusiasm about the pioneer Canadian West. After graduation in 1910, the adventurous young Coldwell accepted an advertised teaching post in New Norway, Alberta, where he lived on a ranch and rode horseback daily to school. He was chosen the next year to be principal of a rural school near Regina because, one story has it, the school board thought that "Major" James William Coldwell could impose a needed military discipline. His bride, Norah, was hired to teach in the same school.

Rural Saskatchewan gave the young couple new insights into the precarious life of farmers, ranchers and homesteaders. Both became increasingly aware that the harsh problems of the Canadian Prairies — where prices, land, loans and markets were often controlled by alien forces and institutions — were vastly different from the bucolic conditions of South Devon.

Already active in community affairs, M. J. headed discussion groups on current issues, and was persuaded to run for alderman in Regina. Norah led women's groups that examined such books as Shaw's *Every Woman's Guide to Socialism*. The concern for social justice had led inexorably to action for political reform.

Besides serving as alderman, Coldwell was elected president of the Canadian Federation of Teachers, president of the Independent Labour Party, and then leader of a new farmer-labour coalition from which the Saskatchewan CCF later emerged.

Recurrent challenges, too many to mention here, tested Coldwell's mettle and moulded his character. The Regina School Board refused him a leave of absence to campaign for municipal office, and ordered him to withdraw his candidacy or face dismissal. In depression-stricken Saskatchewan this was no negligible threat for the head of a family with two small children, an ailing wife and no outside income. Coldwell, always encouraged by the indomitable Norah, refused to cede and was elected.

As a neophyte alderman, he urged that the unemployed receive humane treatment as a matter of right. Early in his term he investigated food supplies for those who were bereft during the winter months after the harvest season. He checked complaints by pretending to be jobless himself and by applying for relief. He found food provisions inadequate. His investigations infuriated city officials, but resulted in the problem's rectification.

In 1935 Coldwell was elected to the federal Parliament, where he joined the small but influential CCF group on the national scene.

During the 1934–35 federal campaign, Canada's senior Catholic prelate, Cardinal Villeneuve, issued an unprecedented pastoral letter warning against socialism and support for CCF candidates. Coldwell replied forthrightly that the new party shared the democratic traditions and goals of similar movements elsewhere in the British Commonwealth.

On September 3, 1939, the German invasion of Poland, preceded by the Nazi-Soviet pact, precipitated the Second World War. To an attentive and respectful House of Commons, the CCF leader, J. S. Woodsworth, a fervent pacifist, explained why he could not personally support the war effort. He resigned as CCF parliamentary leader, and was succeeded by M. J. Coldwell. By late summer of 1940, Western Europe had fallen to the Axis powers while the Soviet Union seized eastern Poland, the Baltic states and parts of Rumania. Britain stood alone in the front line of defence with a coalition government in which the Labour Party was a full partner.

After considerable debate, the Liberal government of Prime Minister Mackenzie King enacted a two-tiered policy: conscription for home defence only, with overseas service to be on a voluntary basis. It was a compromise policy that neither satisfied English-speaking interventionists nor placated French-speaking isolationists. The CCF under Coldwell supported the war effort, but urged that "compulsory mobilization of industry and wealth" must precede conscription of manpower. What the policy meant in practice or how it could be implemented was never really clarified. A leading CCF policymaker, responding to the query of a bemused soldier, answered in a manner befitting a political theorist far removed from imminent danger: "If the Germans land in the Maritimes and the Japanese in British Columbia, we shall still oppose compulsory military service without conscription of wealth and industry."

Those associated with Coldwell soon after the war had good reason to infer that, as a committed internationalist, anti-fascist and believer in a British Commonwealth of free nations, he had become increasingly uncomfortable with an equivocal CCF wartime policy at variance with that of socialist colleagues in countries under siege. His doubts may have crystallized in September 1944, when he travelled to London for a meeting of Commonwealth labour party leaders, and then was invited to visit Canadian military positions in Normandy and Belgium, secured after heavy combat.

Following his return to Ottawa, rising Canadian casualties precipitated a bitter parliamentary debate on whether home service recruits should be sent abroad as reinforcements. Coldwell took a position that reversed CCF policy: "Let us be frank about it; all parties in this House repudiated conscription for overseas service in 1940. Now the support we owe our gallant men in the firing line demands immediate reinforcements. Whatever that support entails should be undertaken." He then introduced a motion authorizing "the immediate removal of all distinctions between drafted and volunteer personnel, thus making the entire home defence army available for reinforcement overseas." It implicitly abandoned the demand for prior conscription of wealth and industry. When the motion was declared out of order, Coldwell won majority approval for an alternative proposal to "aid the government in maintaining a vigorous war effort."

Coldwell was the primary CCF spokesperson on international affairs from the early wartime years. In a major address toward the end of the war, he projected his vision of a peaceful decolonized world with a "Canada conscious of her obligations as a member of the community of nations, and maintaining close cooperation with the peoples of the British Commonwealth. We will lend aid to the elimination of exploitation everywhere. No world and no people can be secure as long as any part of it is denied the right to live in dignity and freedom. " Coldwell was a committed internationalist who believed that Canada as a "middle power" could exercise a meliorative influence between the giant adversarial camps of the United States and the Soviet Union. He was a confirmed democrat who advocated freedom as the political destiny of all peoples. He had no illusions about the nature of the Soviet Union, which he termed a "totalitarian dictatorship," but deplored the rigid anti-communism prevalent in the United States and rejected "any and all forms of cooperation with Canadian communists who seek to destroy us because we are democratic."

Devoid of moral pieties and never pompous, Coldwell was tolerant of the vagaries of others, and never

judgemental about human frailties. He had a wry and
even mischievous sense of humour. Talking to a former
aide some years later, he recounted earlier meetings with
a rising young Quebec lawyer interested in reform and
progressive politics. But, he said with a smile, "Pierre
Trudeau decided the CCF was not radical enough; so he
joined the Liberal Party."

He also had calls and visits from Joseph Smallwood,
then editor of a radical New York review, weighing a
CCF political career when his native Newfoundland
attained provincial status in 1949. Coldwell was not
surprised when Smallwood decided that his ambitions
to become the province's first premier would be more
effectively promoted by the Liberal Party.

There has not yet been a biography that does justice
to Coldwell's signal public contributions and personal
character. It is sorely needed. Coldwell wrote one book,
Left Turn, Canada, and typically said little about himself. Its inscription read: "For my wife — Norah Gertrude Coldwell." Mrs. Coldwell died in 1953, always
brave and dignified throughout her lingering illness.

Elected five times since 1935, Coldwell was defeated
in the Conservative landslide of 1958 at the age of
sixty-nine. He retired from public life with habitual
grace and distinction. He continued to support the CCF,
and served as national chairman until its conversion in
1961 into the New Democratic Party. He then lectured
and taught in Canada and abroad. Opposed as always to
a non-elective deliberative assembly, he declined an
offer by Prime Minister Pearson to sit in the Senate.

M. J. Coldwell died at the age of eighty-five on
August 25, 1974. Only a month previously, he had been
interviewed by the labour press after federal elections in
which the NDP lost fifteen seats. He reiterated his confidence that the party would still become one of

Canada's two major political organizations. Looking back with typical humility, he said: "I'm very proud of the fact that I've been associated with this party and helped to promote its policies and principles. I feel I've been able to make some little contribution to the benefit of my fellow Canadians, and that's all I wanted to do."

This was one time when M. J. Coldwell was in error. He had made no "little" contribution to his fellow citizens. His contribution was immeasurable.

Tommy Douglas

Pierre Berton

I once wrote that had Tommy Douglas not existed he would have had to be invented. Fortunately he did exist — and in the right place at the right time. Few Canadians have left behind more enduring monuments than this scrappy, bantam cock of a man — part practical politician, part idealist, part evangelist, part ham actor.

Of all those monuments, surely the most endearing is universal Medicare. More than anything else, I believe, it is the philosophy behind this social milepost that distinguishes us from the more individualistic community south of the border. Tommy Douglas and his party taught us to be a more caring nation, taught us the value of co-operation as an antidote to untrammelled competition, taught us that the community as a whole has a moral responsibility to the afflicted.

Like Medicare, Douglas's character was forged in the crucible of the Great Depression. No politician who travelled the back roads of southern Saskatchewan in those dark days could fail to be moved by the plight of those who could not afford a doctor, or those doctors who could not afford to treat patients. Actually, the country *could* afford a variety of social programs, as Douglas himself noted. Surely, he declared in 1945, "if we can produce in such abundance in order to destroy our enemies, we can produce in equal abundance in order to provide food, clothing and shelter for our children."

That was certainly true in the matter of health care. When he was fighting his last provincial election against the vested interests represented by the Canadian Medical Association, Douglas made mincemeat of the "we can't afford it" gang by quoting hard figures. The previous year, he pointed out, Canadians had spent twice as much on alcohol and tobacco as on medical and dental care. "I say we ought to have a sufficient sense of values to say that health is more important than these things," he declared, "and if we can find the money for non-essential things, we can find the money to give our people good health."

His fierce determination to ram through the Medicare legislation in Saskatchewan was fuelled by a painful personal memory. As a boy in Winnipeg, suffering from a disease of the bone marrow and unable to pay for specialized medical attention, he faced the loss of a leg. It was saved by happenstance when he was chosen at random from the public ward for a surgical experiment that saved him (and allowed him to go on — always the fighter — to a provincial boxing championship). But why, Douglas asked himself, shouldn't this kind of treatment be available to all, regardless of their ability to pay?

Those pre-Great War days, in Winnipeg, were hard times for the Douglas family. They had come to Canada from Scotland in 1910, when young Tommy was six years old and sickly. They lived in the ferment of the city's North Side — a world of immigrants and social activists of whom J. S. Woodsworth of the All People's Mission was the crowning ornament. The Douglas family returned to Glasgow during the war when Tommy's father joined the British Army. And here the youngster came under the influence of such Labour orators as Keir Hardie.

Back in Winnipeg at the age of thirteen, Tommy Douglas gave up school to help support his family. Later he studied theology at Brandon College and was exposed to the Social Gospel — the activist Christian movement that refused to remain aloof from the problems of humanity. As Douglas put it, "if Christianity means anything, it means building the brotherhood of man." Ordained as a Baptist minister, he honed his oratory in the pulpit — a technique that proved useful when he entered municipal and later provincial politics. Few politicians understood the power of radio in those days, but Douglas did. On the lecture platform and in the rough and tumble of parliamentary debate he was unbeatable. He spoke without notes, making his points with humour — peppering his talk with jokes that were often modern parables and entrancing his audience for whom, in those Depression years, politics was the only theatre.

In 1944, after a stint in Ottawa, and as leader of the provincial CCF, he formed the first democratic socialist government in Canada. The establishment was shaken by his victory. The business world raised millions of dollars to attack the whole idea of a planned economy, which Douglas and the CCF advocated. "Planning" became a dirty word — and this from businessmen who would never erect a building without an architect or open a bank account without a financial plan for their future.

Douglas's idea of planned economy, however, was one "which is planned in the interest of all our citizens and not just for a privileged few." That form of economic democracy was exactly what his opponents were fighting.

He won five provincial elections in succession — a remarkable record — and he changed the face of Saskatchewan. Then, in 1960, he returned to federal politics (which he had originally entered in 1935), as leader of the New Democratic Party, successor to the CCF. For the next decade, Tommy Douglas was the national spokesman for the democratic left in Canada.

He was ever on the side of the angels. He opposed nuclear arms for Canada and scorned the government's vacillation on that thorny issue: a policy of "indecision and timidity," he called it. He was appalled by the Columbia River treaty — "conceived in avarice and born in apathy" — which, in effect, gave the Americans control over Canadian waters. He fought against capital punishment because he believed that "any society that practiced capital punishment brutalizes itself."

He fought for a distinctive flag and told those who kept "talking about the Union Jack, the Battle of Hastings and British history" that they should realize that "we cannot go back into the womb of the past." He tried, vainly, to get the Canadian government to speak out against the bombing of North Vietnam — which he correctly termed "a moral outrage." And he did not subscribe to the establishment view that the Royal Canadian Mounted Police could do no wrong. What he and his party were objecting to, he said in 1963, was that "under the umbrella of seeking to root out subversion we find interference with free speech and an attempt to intimidate people who are exercising their democratic rights."

It is well to remember that these views — which have now been accepted by the establishment — were highly unpopular and that Tommy Douglas was vilified for expressing them. His finest moment came on November 4, 1970, when in the face of almost universal opposition, he and his party opposed the enforcing of the War

Measures Act under which hundreds of innocent Quebec citizens were jailed without the right to *habeas corpus*.

Douglas's speech on that occasion deserves to be etched into the granite of the Centre Block. "Right now there is no constitution in this country," he reminded the House, "no Bill of Rights, no provincial constitutions. The government now has the power by Order in Council to do anything it wants — to intern any citizen, to arrest any person, or to declare any organization subversive or illegal. These are tremendous powers to put into the hands of the men who sit on the Treasury benches ..."

And again: "The government has fallen right into a trap. The government has done exactly what the FLQ hoped they would do. All across this country, students, workers, and alienated groups will be told: 'See what happens when he fights on your behalf? The government immediately brings in repressive measures.' ... I say to the government that we cannot protect democratic freedoms by restricting, limiting and destroying democratic freedoms."

It all seems logical and sensible today. But given the temper of those times, when he was forced to endure the jeers and catcalls of his Liberal and Conservative colleagues, not to mention the fury of most of the nation's press, Douglas's position, stated boldy and publicly, stands as a signal act of courage.

We know now that Tommy Douglas was right. But then he usually was.

Grace and Angus MacInnis

as told by Grace MacInnis to Leo Heaps

Grace MacInnis was the grand lady of the New Democrats. Like her father, J. S. Woodsworth, she was considered an "ornament to Parliament." She served as a member of the House of Commons in Ottawa as well as in the British Columbia Legislature. Grace was the only survivor of that small group who attended the first CCF parliamentary caucus in Ottawa in 1935. Her husband, Angus MacInnis, who was also a member of that first CCF caucus, and Grace were known for speaking with one voice on most major issues. Angus MacInnis served as a federal member of Parliament from 1930 to 1940. Beginning with J. S. Woodsworth, three members of one family held public office almost continuously for fifty-four years. Grace MacInnis's life remains an example of unselfishness.

At age eighty-four in 1991, disabled, in a nursing home alone, Grace was courageous. Her quiet sense of confidence that Canada would create a party able to govern in the image of her ideals was her fondest hope. The following interview took place on November 14, 1990. In it she summed up her principles, which she believed should now guide the New Democratic Party. Grace MacInnis died in July 1991.

"You have to excuse me. But I shall do my best to remember what I have always considered important and what I think New Democrats should stand for. I am forgetting quite a few things these days but I will try to recall those ideas which, in my opinion, are the basis of any political movement of democratic socialism. If some of these ideas appear far-fetched, just think how remote our accomplishments would be regarded, viewed from half a century ago. The dreamers are winning.

"I deplore the spectacular and most of our modern techniques of public relations. I disavow them because I do not believe they have lasting value. And the New Democrats have been an offender. They are avenues which lead to solutions that do not belong to our movement. In the end you cannot fool the people. Our goals are too simple not to be clear to all those who wish to listen to us. In my mind, the message of our party and that of our pioneers and those thousands of men and women who have sacrificed so much has not changed over the years. It is true the times and techniques may have changed, but our message must remain the same.

"The philosophy of the early workers of our party and those others who struggled to free themselves in Europe and distant parts of the world has not changed either. Each generation battles against a system of economic and political tyranny that threatens to stifle and deprive the innocent and unprotected of their rights, whether the threat originates from law established by the courts or whether the threat comes from the manipulation of the marketplace. The methods and sophistication of the approach may vary but the results are the same. The tyranny of the majority can be just as devastating as the cruelty of a dictator. And we must also guard against that. If I remember correctly, and I hope I still do, Alexis de

Tocqueville said that almost a century and a half ago in his observations on America.

"In our society, as in the world, control of wealth is in the hands of fewer and fewer nations, fewer and fewer people and fewer corporations. It makes no difference whether those owners are giant monopolies or individuals, the results are similar. All my life, I have advocated a change in the system whereby the wealth of our land can be returned to the producers of that wealth. I know this belief is not too fashionable among many people, some of whom are members of our own party. But lack of popularity has never bothered me because my eyes were always focused on an ideal far ahead and just over the horizon.

"I also know that not all our dreams are attainable in our lifetime. And then there come those glorious moments when, without warning, the unexpected becomes true and the people of Canada who are coming to our side in larger numbers suddenly acclaim us. And in an instant our dreams become a living reality. Those of you who know me well, and there are probably not too many around anymore, are aware I have never courted popularity. I am an old-time socialist and I will die one. We are very few in number today. Maybe Stanley Knowles, who is still about, would stand with me as well as all that group that sat and had their picture taken in the first caucus in the Commons fifty-five years ago. I am the only one left from that photo. This should make me feel very lonely. And somehow, as I sit in my wheelchair, I feel very proud of my past life and don't feel one bit lonely. My memories, my great associates are around me still. Their spirit surrounds me. J. S. Woodsworth, A. A. Heaps, my dear husband Angus MacInnis, Grant Mac-Neil, J. M. Coldwell, Tommy Douglas, Agnes Macphail and all those hundreds of men and women who kept their belief alive in our darkest hours are still beside me. They are all here. So I am not lonely. I have only to shut my eyes and I am swamped by friends. And that is the way I wish it to be to the last.

"Today members of Parliament are living a different style of life, incomparable to that which I recollect. They are among the affluent of our society. Some don't bother to answer letters anymore. They send printed postcards instead. This is an insult to the constituents. We always had time for a letter and we were just as busy then with much less help, no fax machines and no staff of five or six as some MPs have. I'm not one who looks back to the so-called good old days. They no longer exist. But I do believe life for parliamentarians is much easier than it used to be and they don't accomplish much more than we did. There are more privileges for our elected officials. They are also more regimented than they were and often less responsive to the people until just before election.

"We as a party have no monopoly on morality or honesty. We members of the NDP are no better nor worse than others. Some of us have become very pretentious, as if we know the best way to keep the peace, or to cure the inequalities of society. That is not so. Within our party, like all parties, we have the extremes of opinion, the good and the bad. But always that old dream of a better world keeps nagging us, reminding us amidst all the politicking that we should not lower our sights no matter the enticements of power. We have come as far as we have because the people of Canada believe we are different from the others; that we are more open, that we won't become so self-important that we have no time to respond to a cry for help. If we forget what we are, use the excuse we are too busy to attend to a needy Canadian, then we will have lost our way and it will not be long before there will be no difference between us and the others. That must never happen.

"As you are probably aware, I have been a child of Canadian politics almost since birth. I was weaned in the cradle of politics. And I have abhorred the condition in our society where we suffer from an abundance of too much wealth without the means to distribute that same wealth. Our nation always seems to be confounded by this problem that not only affects Canada, but the world. We in this land have almost too much of everything, yet men and women cannot buy the food and goods because they are unable to work and earn. We have food banks and welfare where we should have work as a means of providing our daily bread. We survivors know that only through reaching for the stars can we achieve our ideal of a humane society where no man or woman is in want, and somewhere there is a place for everyone. That is the ideal. We shall all dedicate ourselves to its achievement. And so I shall dream of that. And as this great movement grows, our aim shall be as true as it was when we were only a handful.

"It is difficult for me to discuss politics without mentioning my late husband, Angus MacInnis, in the same breath. Both of us were children of politics and our life together for over eighteen years was spent almost totally absorbed in the CCF. Angus had been a motorman in Vancouver and later an alderman. He was a simple, straightforward man. But his sound judgement and fund of practical wisdom were inexhaustible and he had a way of healing divisions within our party. He was unshakable, steady as the Rock of Gibraltar, and will be remembered best for his somewhat dour humour and calmness during moments of crisis. Nothing could upset or unnerve Angus. Like some of the early parliamentarians he was largely self-educated. When the CCF voted to oppose J. S. Woodsworth's pacifism in World War II, Angus with great sadness voted against his father-in-law. His view was that you could be a man of peace but the Nazis had to be stopped or the world would descend into a dark age that would devastate civilization. There could be no life without liberty and no liberty without personal sacrifice. His conciliatory character helped knit together the considerable discord in the CCF parliamentary caucus after the party divided on the issue of peace.

"Physically, Angus was rough-hewn, a lean, powerful figure whose voice could roar like thunder. He seemed to blend into the stone of the parliamentary corridors, or, as Tommy Douglas said, 'Angus was quarried from rock.' Although his contribution in terms of major reforms may not have been as outstanding as some of his contemporaries', his quality of character, his absolute integrity of principle and his dedication to the ideals of true democracy gave considerable strength to the small CCF band in Parliament."

Agnes Macphail

Lynn McDonald

Agnes Campbell Macphail was Canada's first and, for many years, only woman MP. She was part of the Progressive contingent — they did not call themselves a party — a farmers' representative in the days when UFO meant United Farmers of Ontario. In Parliament in the 1920s she joined J. S. Woodsworth's Ginger Group that led to the founding of the CCF. She was at the party's founding convention in 1933, although she left it with the UFO the following year. She later returned to organize for the CCF in Ontario and represented it, as the MPP for East York, in the provincial legislature.

Macphail was proud of being of Scottish descent and farm stock. She was born in a three-room log house in Proton Township, Grey County, about thirty miles from Owen Sound. Her maternal family, the Campbells, had been landowners in Scotland, but the Macphails were poor. Her grandfather, head shepherd on a large estate in the western Highlands, immigrated to western Ontario, walking into bleak farmland in Grey County, squatting and then getting title. Agnes went to high school in Owen Sound, normal school in Stratford, and taught in a variety of rural schools. In 1919, while teaching near Sharon (north of Toronto), she began to support the farmers' movement and discovered her gift for speaking. She campaigned for the UFO in the provincial election that year. Then she returned to her home town to make herself available for the next federal election, the first in which Canadian women could vote and run. She won the nomination on the seventh ballot, strongly supported by the men of her township. No women delegates were at that meeting. She was thirty-one when first elected member of Parliament for Southeast Grey in 1921.

Agnes Macphail became an articulate spokesperson for most of the important social causes of the inter-war period. On her death it was said that there had been little good social legislation in which she had not played a part. The list is formidable: prison reform, in which she played a leading role, numerous welfare-state measures, electoral and civil service reform and civil liberties legislation, in addition to advocacy of peace and disarmament. Identifying with her class of origin, she declared that she "would infinitely prefer to raise the class of which I am one than by any means whatever to creep above it or out of it."

There were, however, false starts. Macphail promptly got herself into difficulty by advocating a pay decrease for MPs. The first term she turned back $1500 of the $4000 yearly stipend, but later realized she could easily spend it all and took it. She enjoyed entertaining constituents in Ottawa and her riding, making donations and sponsoring prizes for worthy students. Never a saver, Macphail was poor in her last years. She did speaking tours in the United States to buy herself a pension, but did not live long enough to enjoy it.

If Macphail's first concern was the welfare of the farmers who elected her, she soon found that others, too, needed her attention. One of her speeches in the House was on the plight of Glace Bay miners and their families, protesting the "special privilege and great power" granted to the British Empire Steel Corporation. In 1925 she visited Glace Bay, now with the miners out on a long and bitter strike. Her reports told of malnutrition and anaemia; there were children with no shoes to go to school. Never unsure of where her sympathies lay, Macphail gradually found herself supporting the welfare-state proposals of J. S. Woodsworth and his small caucus. She supported the original old age pension and numerous measures to improve it. As soon as pensions for the blind had been established she advocated pensions for the totally disabled. She sought public support for low-cost housing, arguing that "good housing for all the people is the greatest national investment we can make."

In 1936, Macphail toured Sweden, Denmark and the Soviet Union with a McGill University group led by Leonard Marsh, later author of the report outlining the Canadian welfare state. She returned more than ever a social democrat, now with more and better examples to make the case for government initiatives. Her observations on the Soviet Union were astute.

One of the most difficult causes Macphail took on was prison reform. Federal penitentiaries in the first decades of the century were brutal places where untrained, politically appointed wardens meted out rough justice for infractions of prison rules. There was no due process. She advocated a system of productive work for prisoners. She spoke and wrote against shackling, paddling, sentences of isolation with a bread-and-water diet and flogging, then practised with a strap that tore the skin off the prisoner's back. Insisting on her prerogative as an MP she visited Kingston Penitentiary, including the "hole." She advocated the investigation of the causes of crime and the functioning of penitentiaries. Eventually a royal commission was appointed, and it recommended sweeping changes. Its chair, Joseph Archambault, sent her a copy of the final report in 1938 in appreciation for the role she had played. She continued to press for better treatment and education of prisoners, and training for prison staff. Years later, at her burial, one of the wreaths was from the prisoners of Kingston, with their gratitude.

As early as 1924, Macphail spoke for the abolition of capital punishment, supporting William Irvine's private member's bill on the subject. If we want to teach love, do we hate? she asked. If we are to reverence human life we must refuse to take it.

> Punishment should be of a reforming character rather than revengeful ... to me life is sacred, and because it is such a sacred thing I personally could not take the life of anyone, even though that one had taken the life of another.

Canada's first woman parliamentarian was no feminist. Macphail was a friend of Nellie McClung, who had also been born in Grey County, but Macphail took no part in the suffrage movement and naïvely believed that equality had been achieved with the vote. Making the first trek from the House of Commons to the Senate, for the ceremony of royal assent, she imagined that other women would soon follow: "I could almost hear them coming." Yet it was not until 1936 that another woman was elected, and she was only filling in for a sick husband; she resigned on his recovery. When Macphail was defeated there were again no women in the House.

In her first speech in the House, Macphail set out her belief in equality. She opposed a measure to extend citizenship and the vote to women on the basis of marriage. "Women just want to be individuals, as men are individuals — no more and no less. And so I would like to see that principle embodied in the law, rather than that a woman should be made citizen by marriage to a man who was himself a citizen."

At the founding convention of the CCF, Macphail derided a proposal that "a woman" be a member of each committee:

> I'm sick and tired of this woman business. If I didn't get anything by merit, I didn't want it.

And she walked out! Alas, when she herself was defeated she could not get a job, despite her considerable merits. She was turned down by the federal public service and the Ontario Co-operative Society, and lasted only a year as a columnist with *The Globe and Mail*. The situation was no better after her two provincial defeats, in 1945 and 1951; she took in boarders.

On any issue of equality Macphail could be counted on; not for nothing was the UFO's motto "equality for all, special privilege for none." Macphail thus supported equal pay for equal work in the provincial legislature, while in Parliament she had spoken for equal rights to divorce, domicile and citizenship. She understood the double burden on women and deplored the double standard. "It is a fact that all women contribute more to marriage than men," she explained in 1925, noting that it was they who changed their names and often also their place of living and their occupation on marriage, then went to work without wages until death. She had early decided not to marry because she wanted to make her own contribution to life as a *person*. She turned down a number of proposals, two from fellow MPs. One unhappy suitor remained single for life. Amongst her correspondence at the Public Archives are valentines to "sweet Aggie," for she did not want history to know her as a frustrated old maid. She flirted with R. B. Bennett, exchanging notes as "Sir Richard" and "Dame Agnes."

History records few better statements on equality in marriage than hers:

> I do not want to be the angel of any home; I want for myself what I want for other women, absolute equality. After that is secured then men and women can take turns at being angels.

The preservation of the home, she argued in another speech, lay in the hands of men:

> If they are willing to give to women economic freedom within that home; if they are willing to live by the standard that they wish women to live by, the home will be preserved. If the preservation of the home means the enslavement of women, economically or morally, then we had better break it.

A committed peace activist for two decades, when the decision was made for Canada to join Britain in war in 1939 she was silent. Macphail had been a member of the Women's International League for Peace and Freedom and was a delegate to international meetings. She marched for peace outside the House and spoke for it within. She voted for lower military spending and active disarmament. A great power could not disarm so easily as we could, she conceded, but disarmament could be Canada's contribution to world peace. She opposed military training for boys in school, arguing instead for physical training for both sexes. Cadet training was *not* good physical training, it confused the regimental spirit with the co-operative, and it prevented young people from developing free ideals. She decried Empire Day celebrations as the "flaunting of war." Yet, in her last speech in the House of Commons, she did not address the question of war itself. Instead she argued for good farm prices and described her pessimism about Canada's future. She was defeated in the 1940 election, leaving Canada without a single woman MP, and again in a by-election in Saskatchewan soon after. Friends were rallying to get her a Senate appointment when she died in 1954.

Macphail is remembered as a powerful speaker, a tall figure with a deep voice that carried far. She was quick with hecklers, although her biographers could not verify one of the more popular anecdotes. Male heckler: "Don't you wish you were a man?" Macphail: "Yes, don't you?" When I first ran for Parliament in Broadview-Greenwood, I met East Yorkers who remembered her fondly as their MPP. I had been told that a woman could not win the riding — in 1982 no less — but these people told me they would have no difficulty voting for a woman for they had voted for Agnes Macphail!

Stanley Knowles

Larry Wagg and Leo Heaps

Stanley Knowles was born on June 18, 1908, in Los Angeles, California, of middle-class parents. His father came from Nova Scotia and his mother from New Brunswick. At the age of sixteen he decided to come to Canada on his own to attend Brandon College, and then the United College in Winnipeg and the University of Manitoba. He received his degree at Brandon in 1930 and later graduated as Bachelor of Divinity in Winnipeg in 1934. An outstanding student, he won proficiency medals and numerous other awards during his academic years.

For thirty-eight years he served as a member of Parliament for Winnipeg North Centre, J. S. Woodsworth's old seat, with one short break between 1958 and 1962. When he was not attending to his parliamentary duties, Stanley served as a member of Local 191, International Typographical Union, or as a minister of the United Church of Canada. In 1967 he was made an Honorary Fellow of United College. In the same year, Brandon University awarded him a Doctor of Laws degree at its first convocation, a degree which was also given to him by McMaster University in 1972; Queen's University and the University of Toronto in 1976; Trent University in 1978; and York University in 1979. In July 1970, Stanley Knowles was installed as Chancellor of Brandon University; he continued in this role for twenty years.

For this one-time printer the honours poured in, after a long life of service to his country.

As one reminisces on the long years of impressive accomplishments of Stanley Knowles, one feels that there lies within the character of this man the same strong sense of dedication that directed the life of J. S. Woodsworth. Always he has endeavoured to represent the best in politics, from the time he chaired the first national conventions of the Co-operative Commonwealth Federation until his days ended as an active member of Parliament.

Knowles gained considerable experience in the realm of foreign affairs and was chosen as early as 1945 as a member of the Canadian delegation to the United Nations Preparatory Commission in London, as well as a delegate to the first session of the United Nations General Assembly in that same city in 1946. His contributions became more and more notable as his international experience widened. Knowles's colleagues could always count upon his solid common-sense approach to any situation.

In 1957 Stanley was approached by Prime Minister Diefenbaker and asked if he would become Speaker of the House, since he was among the few who had enjoyed the respect of all the Commons. The honour was declined, since Stanley preferred to carry on his efforts to improve the lot of the people of Canada while he sat as a parliamentarian. (A copy of the Prime Minister's letter was later tabled in the House, for the record.) Ironically, Stanley was defeated in Winnipeg North Centre by a Progressive Conservative candidate in the general election held the following year, but he continued his work on behalf of old age pensioners and veterans, which he considered a top priority. At the founding convention of the Canadian Labour Congress he became executive vice-president, being re-elected for another two years in 1960. Knowles was also one of the main architects of the New Democratic Party: he was elected chairman of the interim committee for the New Party, which led eventually to the formation of the New Democratic Party. In his book, *The New Party,* he laid down the principles and goals of this political movement.

In 1962 Stanley returned to his first love, the House of Commons, as the New Democratic member for Winnipeg North Centre, his old CCF constituency. He needed Parliament as much as Parliament needed him. For almost a decade this venerable citizen acted as House leader of the New Democrats and as chief whip until November 30, 1979, his thirty-seventh year in Ottawa. On this day Parliament made an exceptional gesture by making Stanley Knowles a member of the Privy Council of Canada. In a way he had become a national treasure.

In June 1981, Parliament voted its members a substantial increase in salary at a time when the country was in recession and interest rates were destroying the lives of hundreds of thousands of Canadians. The government was asking citizens to tighten their belts. The entire New Democratic Party in the Commons voted for a salary increase except Stanley Knowles. He was one of two parliamentarians in the House who believed MPs made enough and were setting a bad example for the nation. By and large, he said, NDP members were making more money than they had done in private life, enjoyed more privileges, and had sufficient financial advantages at their present level of pay to do all the work they had to do. This was not the only occasion on which he opposed an increase in the pay of MPs.

That same year Stanley Knowles was struck suddenly by a paralysing stroke that removed him from an active role in Parliament. But neither Parliament nor Prime Minister Pierre Trudeau could forget this modest, quiet statesman. On March 13, 1984, Trudeau, supported by all members in the House, made a motion conferring upon Stanley the unprecedented status of Honorary Officer of the House. It would no longer be necessary for Stanley to endure the political rigours of election campaigns. After thirty-eight years, his place in the Commons was assured with a seat at the table for as long as he lived.

To this day Stanley Knowles appears each afternoon in the Commons at his chair at the grand table, a reminder to the House that there are greater things in life than the machinations of politics and the ambitions of power and office. There is service and compassion.

David Lewis

Alan Whitehorn

David Lewis was baptized into the world of politics at a
very early age. Born a member of the Losh family
(Lewis's original family name) in the small Jewish village of Svisloch in Tsarist Russia in the year 1909, the
young David lived through the German invasion of
Russia in the First World War and the Russian Revolution of 1917. During this time, David's father, Moishe,
a radical political activist, was condemned to death by
the Bolsheviks. While his father's life was eventually
spared, the incident left the young Lewis with a "deep
and lasting animosity toward all communists." With
prospects increasingly bleak in the East European town,
the Losh family immigrated to a safer land.

The family, now renamed Lewis, arrived in Montreal
in 1921. Although David was unable to speak English
initially, armed with a copy of Dickens's *The Old Curi-
osity Shop* and characteristic determination, the young
immigrant soon mastered the new language. As Lewis's
education progressed, his public speaking skills were
honed to the point that he became an accomplished
speaker and a devastating debater at McGill University
and in the local labour parties.

His experiences in both Europe and Canada led Lewis
to see political and social relations in terms of class
inequality and struggle. In this regard, Lewis was more

inclined to employ confrontational language than J. S. Woodsworth and others who were from the social gospel tradition. The latter approach, he believed, was too optimistic and idealistic in its hopes of a co-operative path to the New Jerusalem. Similarly, in international affairs, Lewis rejected the utopianism of Woodsworth's pacifism in favour of a more realistic policy of collective security.

One of the most important influences on David Lewis was a small group of Canadian academics in the League for Social Reconstruction (LSR). These Fabian-style socialists included Frank Scott, Frank Underhill, Eugene Forsey, and others. It was Scott who encouraged the young and impoverished undergraduate to apply for the prestigious Rhodes scholarship.

Davis Lewis's interview for the Rhodes scholarship is now part of the annals of Canadian political folklore. Among the members of the examining committee was Sir Edward Beatty, the president of the CPR, one of Canada's largest and most powerful corporations. After forty-five minutes of questioning by the committee, Sir Edward Beatty turned to Lewis and posed this question: "Lewis, if you became the first socialist prime minister of Canada, what would be the first thing you would do?" With a "defiant glint" in his eyes, Lewis shot back: "Nationalize the CPR, sir." Lewis won his scholarship.

The years at Oxford, England (1932–1935), enabled Lewis to establish close contacts with members of the British Labour Party. Lewis's prominence was such that he was offered a law practice and a safe Labour Party seat in Britain. While Lewis was studying at Oxford, he was also in contact with J. S. Woodsworth (1874–1942), federal leader of the newly created CCF. Woodsworth encouraged Lewis to return to Canada. After a brief stint working in an Ottawa law office, David Lewis commenced work as the part-time national secretary of the CCF in 1936 and opened the party's new and modest headquarters in Ottawa. It lacked a washroom and had only a sand floor. Within two years the party's national office expanded and Lewis was hired as full-time national secretary, a role in which he would continue until 1950.

In the 1940s, Frank Scott and David Lewis emerged as high-profile spokespersons for the national CCF and co-authored *Make This Your Canada*. A remarkable 25 000 copies of this book were sold in less than one year. In the same year, 1943, the CCF briefly led in the national public opinion polls and made spectacular electoral gains to become the Official Opposition in Ontario. A year later it formed the government in Saskatchewan. Many expected that the federal CCF would also achieve an electoral breakthrough. It was not to be, however, as the forces of big business launched a multi-million dollar anti-socialist campaign. One of the targets, not surprisingly, was the CCF's high-profile national secretary, David Lewis.

In 1950, with CCF prospects dwindling and faced with the need to ease his family's financial burdens, Lewis stepped down as national secretary and opted to practise labour law in Toronto with Ted Joliffe, who was Ontario CCF leader from 1942 to 1953. Working heavily on labour legal cases, the dynamic Lewis was able to widen his already extensive contacts with senior trade union officials and in so doing strengthen the links between the struggling CCF and the growing and increasingly unified labour movement. Lewis's contacts would prove crucial in the formation of the New Democratic Party. During the 1940s and early 1950s, Lewis also endeavoured to lessen the influence in the trade union movement of Communist followers of

Stalin. And he kept up an active role in the CCF. From the 1950s onwards, Lewis served in a number of the party's senior executive positions. He was a key figure in the drafting of both the Winnipeg Declaration of 1956 and the New Party Statement of Principles in 1961.

In the more than half-century history of the CCF-NDP, few events have been as important as the transformation of the CCF into the NDP in 1961. This phoenix-like rebirth of Canadian socialism was a complex and lengthy process, with its beginnings in the mid-1950s. The Diefenbaker landslide of 1958, however, hastened the process — in that year the CCF and the Canadian Labour Congress (CLC) publicly called for the building of a new "broadly based people's movement."

For Lewis, the goals in creating the New Party involved a triple strategy. One element was to cement the linkages between the labour movement (CLC) and the social democrats (CCF) through the co-sponsorship of a new joint party, the NDP. Lewis, as an architect of the New Party, was also aware that too few Canadians were socialists. Thus, he and his colleagues on the National Committee for a New Party (NCNP) reasoned that as their second objective they must win over the progressive elements of the liberally minded and widen the base of any new party to include more support from the middle class. These had been among the goals of Woodsworth in the founding of the CCF in the 1930s, and were still unfulfilled.

Another crucial goal for the party was to achieve a breakthrough in the key province of Quebec. This Catholic Church-dominated rural province was undergoing a profound social transformation (the "Quiet Revolution") into a more modern, secular and urban society. New Party strategists hoped the new Quebec would be more friendly to social democrats. Accordingly, the New Party stressed its bilingual composition and sensitivity to French-Canadian nationalism.

Despite pleas by a number of party activists for Lewis to lead the New Party, Lewis declined, in large part because he had been a target of antisemitic outbursts during the big-business financed anti-socialist campaign of the 1943–1945 period. Thus Lewis deferred to the very successful Tommy Douglas, who had been premier of Saskatchewan from 1944 to 1961. While Tommy Douglas became the first NDP federal leader, David Lewis was recognized as the architect of the New Democratic Party. It was in many ways "the party that David built."

After unsuccessful attempts at election as a CCF candidate in 1940, a 1943 by-election, 1945, and 1949, Lewis finally gained entry to the House of Commons as a New Democratic MP in 1962. Although he lost again a year later in 1963, he strung together consecutive victories in 1965, 1968 and 1972. Lewis reached the apex of the NDP when he was elected federal leader over Waffle candidate Jim Laxer at the 1971 leadership convention. However, it was a polarized and difficult leadership race, followed by continued factionalism within the party that ultimately reached a climax with the Ontario provincial council's ultimatum in 1972 to the Marxist-inspired Waffle to disband as an organization. With the departure of the Waffle, Lewis was able to turn his attention to Liberal Prime Minister Pierre Trudeau. He looked forward to the challenge. In 1969, Lewis had portrayed Trudeau's arrogance with the following barb: "There but for the grace of Pierre Elliott Trudeau sits God."

Campaigning in 1972 on the inspired theme of no government handouts to "corporate welfare bums,"

Lewis captivated a nation. It was his finest hour of political oratory. While a Liberal minority government emerged, it could survive only as long as Lewis's New Democrats, which held the balance of power, chose to support it. Accordingly, the Liberals would have to address the New Democrats' legislative agenda. David Lewis was at the pinnacle of his political career. This minority Parliament enacted important legislation concerning election expenses, pension indexing, and the creation of Petro-Canada and the Foreign Investment Review Agency.

Minority governments can be difficult for third parties. The 1974 election campaign saw many New Democrat MPs go down to defeat. Even more humbling was the personal defeat of party leader David Lewis. Rather than seeking re-election in a by-election elsewhere, Lewis chose a gracious exit and resigned as federal NDP leader effective 1975. Almost immediately, he began work on his memoirs, *The Good Fight*. It had been all too short a career in the House of Commons, but David Lewis achieved a reputation as one of Canada's finest parliamentarians. More importantly, by his hard work and intelligent guidance, David Lewis helped to forge the New Democratic Party, a highly successful heir to the CCF. As a result, Canadian social democracy continues to flourish.

J.S. Woodsworth, MP and leader of the Co-operative Commonwealth Federation from 1932 to 1942.
Photo courtesy National Archives of Canada / C34443

A.A. Heaps, MP from 1925 to 1940.
Photo courtesy National Archives of Canada / C46920

M.J. Coldwell, MP and leader of the Co-operative Commonwealth Federation from 1942 to 1960.
Photo courtesy National Archives of Canada / C1275

Tommy Douglas, MP from 1935 to 1944 and 1962 to 1979, premier of Saskatchewan from 1944 to 1961, and first leader of the New Democratic Party of Canada from 1961 to 1971.
Photo courtesy National Archives of Canada / C36220

Grace MacInnis, MP from 1965 to 1974 and member of the Legislative Assembly of British Columbia from 1941 to 1945.
Photo courtesy National Archives of Canada / PA 129840

Agnes Macphail, MP from 1921 to 1940, MPP from 1943 to 1948, the first woman to sit in the House of Commons and in the Ontario provincial legislature.
Photo courtesy National Archives of Canada / C21557

Stanley Knowles, MP from 1942 to 1958 and 1962 to 1984, executive vice-president of the Canadian Labour Congress and Canadian delegate to the United Nations.
Photo courtesy National Archives of Canada / PA47354

David Lewis, MP from 1962 to 1974 and leader of the New Democratic Party of Canada from 1971 to 1974.
Photo courtesy National Archives of Canada / PA113483

Tony Penikett, premier of
the Yukon Territories.

Mike Harcourt, MLA and
leader of the British Columbia New Democratic Party.

Ray Martin, MLA and leader of the Alberta New Democratic Party.

Roy Romanow, MLA and leader of the Saskatchewan New Democratic Party.

Gary Doer, MLA and leader of the Manitoba New Democratic Party.

Bob Rae, premier of the province of Ontario and leader of the Ontario New Democratic Party.

Elizabeth Weir, leader of
the New Brunswick New
Democratic Party.

Alexa McDonough,
MLA and leader of the
Nova Scotia New
Democratic Party.

Cle Newhook, leader of the Newfoundland and Labrador New Democratic Party.

Larry Duchesne, leader of the Prince Edward Island New Democratic Party.

The Honourable Ed Broadbent, president of the International Centre for Human Rights and Democratic Development.

The Honourable Audrey McLaughlin, MP and leader of the New Democratic Party of Canada.

Part II
The Nation

The Roots and Evolution of the New Democratic Party

Kenneth McNaught

What the fathers of Canadian socialism saw about them as Canada prepared to enter the twentieth century was a scene of contrasts reminiscent of Charles Dickens's England. Hundred of thousands of immigrants from the British Isles and Europe were pouring into the country, providing the human sinews of rapid growth in the towns, in the mines and forests, and across the vast grain-growing prairies. These men and women built the foundations of our industrialized Canada. Most of them, as well as many thousands of Canadian-born workers, endured lives of savage hardship. With no legal protection for labour unions, without unemployment insurance or any of the pension and welfare structure we know today, they found themselves at the mercy of an unregulated capitalism.

A well-established business-professional class presided over governments at all levels. Free-wheeling banks and other financial institutions profited enormously from the building and operation of mines, mills, tenements, railways, and the filling of the last farming frontiers. The owners and managers of this Canadian version of the Industrial Revolution saw little need to do more than support private charities as they commissioned mansions in Rothsay, Westmount, Rosedale, Wellington Crescent or Shaughnessy Heights. In 1903 the Liberal Sir Wilfrid Laurier proclaimed that the twentieth century belonged to Canada. Already, many thousands of Laurier's compatriots were asking, Whose Canada? What kind of Canada?

The most prominent among those who questioned the merit of the present economic system had come from the British Isles, or had followed events there closely. They were graduates of the struggle in Britain to organize and gain protection for labour unions; they learned, too, the need to organize politically. Nearly defenceless against the decisions of owner-managers with respect to wages, working conditions and job security, these people gave strength to fledgling Canadian unions. They used the arguments developed by the experience of the British unions. In towns across the country local trades and labour councils sought solidarity within what was clearly (if not exactly, in the Marxian sense) a working class. In strikes which were more often lost than won they experienced the full force of "constitutional authority." Laws of contract and the property rights of owner-managers, laws restricting "combinations" of working people, suppression by the police and, not infrequently, the army, led inexorably to political conclusions. Somehow governments would have to be compelled to implement social and economic democracy. Political democracy would have to be remoulded to ensure that governments would cease to be the protectors only of those who owned the country's "private" economic institutions.

The people who risked the wrath of bosses and governments to organize unions and tiny socialist parties bore names such as Pettigrew, Russell, Dixon, Farmer, Simpson, McLaughlin. They had brought with them to

Canada grand notions of a just society, ideas propounded by those British socialists who were busy in the groups that finally came together in 1906 as the Labour Party. While their definitions of socialism and their perceptions of the "class struggle" varied, they had in common a view of society which can best be described as conservative. They accepted literally the term "Industrial Revolution" and they wished to undo it in many ways. They saw that revolution, long accomplished in the "old country," as one which had destroyed the sense of community, robbed artisans of ownership and control of the means of production, driven countless farmers from their land and created huge urban areas of insecurity and destitution. In a very real sense these pioneer Canadian socialists wished to restore and then conserve a society in which governments would ensure a commonwealth rather than merely protect the privileges of property and private wealth.

That our early socialists could and did draw upon ancient British notions of a commonwealth and that they waged their struggles within a flexible parliamentary system is of first importance. These two circumstances explain why a democratic socialist party emerged and grew strong in Canada while political socialism in the United States was still-born. The double Canadian advantage was made clear very early.

In 1903 the Socialist Party of Canada, closely identified with militant unions in mines, forests and dockyards, won a "balance of power" (with two members) in the British Columbia Legislature. The party's house leader, J. W. Hawthornthwaite, faced a dilemma. His decision was to "take advantage of every opportunity of introducing any reforms whatsoever that may be of even temporary benefit to the working man." Hewing to this practical principle, Hawthornthwaite and his colleague,

Parker Williams, talked turkey with the precariously perched Tory Premier Richard McBride. In return for their votes in the legislature they received important improvements in the condition of labour, including the eight-hour day in mines and smelters. This balance of power advantage on other occasions as well made substantial gains in social legislation.

While Canadian socialism would continue to have its left wing, its dominant majority was to remain pragmatic. The majority and the minority agreed that an unrestricted right to private ownership of the "means of production, distribution and exchange" would have to go. They disagreed on the pace, method and extent by which the "profit motive" should be replaced by social ownership and the co-operative ethos. But many socialists knew in the long run this was neither practical nor wise. Direct action (violent revolution followed by total state ownership of economic organizations) has invariably been rejected. Tommy Douglas — who once remarked that the goal of his CCF government was "capitalism with a human face" — knew that his form of socialism had to be adapted to the mores of the new world.

Many industrial workers felt the impact of a political system that operated only for the benefit of the owners. Across the prairies thousands of farm families, often not long away from their original sod houses, saw their slender profits eaten away by mortgage, insurance and banking corporations, while the privately owned railways and grain-handling companies ensured legislative support for their own lucrative operations. In Manitoba, Saskatchewan and Alberta, United Farmers' associations sprang up to challenge eastern business control of the two major parties and to ameliorate the farmers' conditions. The western United Farmers' movement (there were similar groups in other provinces) achieved many immediate goals. Farmers' associations established networks of mutual help, political education and political action groups to field "progressive" candidates who would be responsible to constituency associations rather than to central party organizations. The United Farmers also launched important co-operative activities including a farmer-owned grain-handling company. These, together with a strong co-operative movement in the Maritimes (the "Antigonish Movement") would add much to the grass-roots characteristic of CCF-NDP thinking and action. Just after the end of the First World War, United Farmers formed governments in Alberta and Ontario and elected some sixty-five Progressives to the House of Commons.

While the interests of farmers and industrial workers did not always coincide (with respect to tariffs on manufactures, for example) their mutual concerns were clear enough. So were their ultimate goals and the process by which those goals might be reached. The essential linkage was disillusionment with the artificial doctrine of *laisser-faire*. They perceived all around them the contradictions in a system which encouraged governments to protect corporate rights and privileges while turning a blind eye to human and community rights. They were not deceived by Tory and Liberal politicians who proclaimed the virtues of free competition and individual initiative on a "level playing field." Thus the farmers' Progressive platforms came quickly to resemble those of the small labour and socialist parties of the towns. The farmers called for public ownership of railways and communications, natural resources, hydro-electric power and coal mines, direct government support of co-operatives, steeply graded income and corporation taxes, curtailment of the chartered banks' control of credit and a number of other reforms. Although most of the farmers' platforms stopped short of the socialist demand for nearly complete public ownership of the means of production, they were major building blocks in the evolution of Canadian social democracy.

At the core of the Labour-Farmer political thrust was the conviction that the old-party devotion to competition as an absolute principle was obnoxious as a theory and a sham in practice. As practised, competition turned out to be government support for the elimination of competition, for the protection of financial and industrial monopolies and the view that labour unions were what the common law then said they were: "combinations in restraint of trade."

Economic action alone (through unions, strikes and co-operatives) was not enough to redress the social devastation of capitalism. This was the sermon of a large number of clergymen who articulated a social gospel, arguing for the salvation of souls and communities in *this* world. Calling for establishment of "the Kingdom" here and now, the social gospellers saw church-centred charity as totally inadequate and demanded strong governmental intervention in economic life — an acceptance of responsibility for the well-being of ordinary Canadians. A number of these ministers either loosened or severed their church connections to enter directly into the work of building a democratic socialist party. Their ranks included such prominent pioneers of the CCF-NDP as J. S. Woodsworth, Tommy Douglas, Stanley Knowles, William Irvine, Salem Bland and William Ivens. The ideas of the social gospel influenced many pragmatic labour leaders, such as James Simpson of Toronto who would become in 1934 the first CCF mayor of that city. Widely influential in the farmers' movement, also, the social gospel served as a bridge between the sometimes diverging interests of town and country.

At the end of the First World War a series of strikes exploded across Canada. All were triggered by the tough anti-unionism of employers and governments; all were embittered by wartime profiteering, a soaring cost of living and fears that the war for democracy was resulting in a return to the inequities and sham democracy of the pre-war years. The biggest labour action came in Winnipeg in the spring of 1919 over union recognition and the high cost of living.

Legendary in the history of socialism and unionism, the Winnipeg strike brought the city's economic life to a halt for six weeks. The government feared that the strikers' committee had usurped constituted authority and become the agent of a Bolshevik-Soviet revolution in Canada. In fact, the strike leadership maintained a policy of strict non-violence. Anticipating defeat, Winnipeg businessmen and their lawyers prevailed upon a very compliant Tory government in Ottawa to send in the Mounties and the army. The strike was crushed. Ten strike leaders were arrested and charged with seditious conspiracy or seditious libel. Of the six who were convicted and jailed, three were elected to the Manitoba legislature in 1920 while still in prison. One who was acquitted was elected to Parliament.

Like the Progressive farmers, who also confronted the entrenched political power of business, militant workers drew a political lesson from the industrial turmoil of 1919. Across the country, support for independent labour and socialist parties grew steadily, if unevenly. In Toronto, progressive-minded professional people established a monthly journal, the *Canadian Forum,* whose support for the political left grew steadily throughout the twenties and thirties. In Winnipeg, socialist and labour parties made unprecedented gains in the provincial election of 1920, and the Independent Labour Party became a force in politics.

The ILP platform drew heavily upon the social-economic analysis developed by the Fabian Society and the Labour Party in Britain. Yet while calling for public ownership of the means of production, it did not place the heaviest stress in its election campaign upon dogma. With the slogan "Human Needs Before Property Rights," the ILP pressed for immediate measures such as unemployment insurance, legal security for collective bargaining, revision of the criminal code to ensure freedom of speech, and protection of natural resources from corporate exploitation — in short, for the restructuring of the country as a genuine commonwealth.

By the early thirties the capitalist system was no longer functioning properly. Hundreds of thousands of Canadians were unemployed. One out of every four was without work in Montreal. In 1932 the country's scattered socialists converged to found the Co-operative Commonwealth Federation. Organized by the Ginger Group, the party's founding conference took place in Calgary. Representatives from provincial farmer-labour and socialist parties and radical farm organizations, as well as A. R. Mosher, president of the country's largest railway union (CBRE-ACCL), drew up a short program calling for security of farmers' land tenure, broad social security legislation, a government-operated health service, "social ownership and control of financial institutions, utilities and natural resources," and a "planned economy." A national council was chosen with J. S. Woodsworth as president, and an organizing campaign went forward briskly, directed by experienced leaders such as M. J. Coldwell, E. J. Garland, Louise Lucas, Norman Priestly, Angus MacInnis and Agnes Macphail.

From the outset the CCF was a grass-roots party, as much a people's movement as a political instrument. Almost spontaneously CCF clubs sprouted across the country to discuss policy and draw in existing citizens' groups. Important support came from urban professional people who directed the *Canadian Forum* and, in 1932, founded the League for Social Reconstruction (LSR). Social gospellers such as C. H. Huestis and Salem Bland published regular supportive columns in the *Toronto Star* which, then as now, was the only big newspaper to view democratic socialism with less than abject terror.

The core of the LSR was a group of professors and other professional people, which included such high profiles as F. R. Scott, F. H. Underhill, E. A. Forsey, J. King Gorgon, E. A. Hevelock, G. M. A. Grube, Graham and Irenee Spry and Leonard Marsh. Putting their jobs on the line (businessmen leaned heavily upon their employers to fire them for daring to become politically active) these people were, in a very real sense, the intellectual advance guard of the NDP. They gave lively evidence of their rejection of a class-dominated society, whether governed by Liberals or Conservatives, or advocated by communists. In 1935 the LSR published *Social Planning for Canada*, still the most penetrating analysis of the political economy of the Depression years; it was an LSR committee that produced the working draft of the Regina Manifesto which, with some amendments in convention, was adopted by the first national meeting of the CCF in 1933.

Confirming the worst fears of those who suffered not at all in the dirty thirties, the manifesto idyllically proclaimed:

We aim to replace the present capitalist system with its inherent injustices and inhumanity by a social order in which economic planning will supersede unregulated private enterprise and competition, and in which genuine democratic self-government will be possible.... What we seek is a proper collective organization of our economic resources such as will make possible a much greater degree of leisure and a much richer individual life for each citizen.

The 1933 manifesto was a fighting document for a decade of disaster. In 1956 a CCF convention replaced it with the Winnipeg Declaration. That declaration reflected the thinking and experience of democratic socialists in Europe and New Zealand as well as careful observation of the Canadian context. While the 1956 declaration down-played overly centralized economic planning and accepted the basic elements of a mixed economy, it reasserted vigorously the need to extend social security and to ensure positive government intervention in economic life. The socialist goal of a true commonwealth was in no way diluted.

By 1961 the small bands of CCF MPs at Ottawa and in provincial capitals from Victoria to Toronto were seen not only as the real opposition but as a threat sufficiently serious to secure from both levels of government major advances toward a more just society: security for union organizing and collective bargaining, further development of the welfare state through pension improvements, family allowances, unemployment insurance and progressive labour and welfare legislation. Leaving no doubt about the influence of the socialist political threat, Mackenzie King confided to his diary in 1943: "What I fear is we will begin to have defections from our ranks in the house to the CCF."

The thunder-on-the-left was not to be confined merely to effective parliamentary criticism and advocacy. In 1944 Tommy Douglas, an outspoken social gospeller who in 1935 had been the youngest MP, moved back to Saskatchewan where he led the CCF to victory and formed North America's first socialist government. That government pioneered many public programs such as public-owned auto insurance and giving Crown corporations a new mandate to serve the people — not a few of which were emulated in other provinces. Douglas also put in place Canada's first public health insurance program. Despite very determined opposition from many doctors, Saskatchewan's health scheme was so obviously popular and necessary the Pearson Liberals were virtually compelled to adopt it as a model for the federal Medicare legislation of 1966.

By the end of the fifties the CCF had become a fixture of Canadian political life, boasting some of the country's most respected leaders, such as M. J. Coldwell, Stanley Knowles and David Lewis, all prominent on the Canadian political scene. Although the party appeared to move forward (and backward) in bursts of political success, it seemed unable to break through a kind of electoral sound barrier of less than 15 percent of national voters. The newly forming NDP decided to negotiate what similar parties around the world had found essential — an organic link with labour.

For years such a strategy had been mooted. As early as 1938, District 26 (Nova Scotia) of the United Mine Workers had affiliated with the CCF. But powerful influences made the strategy of an official link with labour difficult. One barrier was the communists who had a strong hold in some major unions. They saw democratic socialism as an impediment to their plan for "true socialism" in a workers' state. Against the communist cadres in the unions, democratic socialist leaders such as Larry Sefton, Charles Millard, Eileen Tallman, William Mahoney, Murray Cotterrill and Fred Dowling finally prevailed. Their success led to the amalgamation of the traditionally conservative Trades and Labour Congress with the more militant Canadian Congress of Labour to form the Canadian Labour Congress in 1956. Establishment of the CLC meant that direct union participation in a political party was now becoming much closer.

Another hindrance to union co-operation was the long-standing influence of the "Gompers tradition" in most Canadian international unions. Sam Gompers, president of the American Federation of Labour for some forty years, entrenched the dogma that unions should be politically non-partisan, simply rewarding their friends and punishing their enemies in the Republican and Democratic parties. Even the political action committees established by CIO unions in the thirties and the later amalgamation of the AFL-CIO brought no substantial change in this flawed reasoning. By the late fifties, democratic socialist leaders in the CLC were prepared to challenge directly the political ideology of their American headquarters. They rejected categorically U.S. labour's non-partisan doctrine, adhering instead to a British-European tradition. In so doing they were to entrench still further Canada's multiparty political structure and confirm an important ingredient of the country's sense of identity.

Spurred on by the disaster of Diefenbaker's electoral sweep in 1958, CCF and CLC leaders began conversations which led to the founding of the New Democratic Party. Important in these preliminaries were Stanley Knowles, Eamon Park, David Lewis and Claude Jodoin. What these leaders and their many colleagues proposed — creation of a new party parented by the CLC and the

CCF — was quickly endorsed by a process very similar to the founding of the CCF. "New Party" clubs sprang up across the country and a series of larger seminars gave shape to the daring political initiative. In the summer of 1961 in Ottawa's steamy Coliseum, some 2000 delegates from the clubs, unions and the CCF debated a draft program that an organizing committee had drawn together from the preceding grass-roots discussions. That program, as amended in convention, together with a party constitution, was adopted and remains the cornerstone of the New Democratic Party.

The NDP was born of compromise; both its pragmatism and its devotion to genuine social democracy, however, reflect its origins in pioneer militant unionism and the CCF vision of a society profoundly dedicated to security and equality for all citizens. New Democrats, like their socialist forerunners, have been the country's effective opposition and have also used minority government situations many times to achieve major social advances. Steadily, the party has built upon that record, becoming not just the credible alternative government but also the actual government — in British Columbia, Saskatchewan, Manitoba and Ontario. At Ottawa the leadership of Tommy Douglas (1961–71), David Lewis (1971–75) and Ed Broadbent (1975–90) as well as the early achievements of the pioneers has had the cumulative effect of placing their successor, Audrey McLaughlin, at the top of federal public opinion polls. In Ontario, the election of September 1990 gave power to the NDP and Bob Rae became premier of the country's most populous province.

The crusading efforts of several generations of Canadian democratic socialists, often enduring serious personal hazards and sacrifice, have made Canada a superior welfare state. They have also nourished a dis-

tinctive political tradition: conservative in its wish to
re-establish the sense of community that has been so
seriously diminished by an unregulated profit motive,
and progressive in its confidence that the parliamentary
system can respond effectively to people's needs and
aspirations.

Labour and the New Democratic Party

Larry Wagg

"Trade union interest in the political life of this country is not something new. The action of the Canadian Labour Congress, at its 1958 convention at Winnipeg, in calling for a political realignment and in taking the first steps toward the formation of the New Party, was not a beginning, it was a culmination."
— *The New Party,* by Stanley Knowles (1961)

Political action has long been familiar to the trade unions. As early as 1898 the unions were advocating free education for all, public ownership of railways, telegraphs, waterworks and lighting, and calling for the abolition of child labour, and for a minimum wage, government inspection of industry and legislation requiring employers to bargain collectively with their employees. The unions also campaigned for the abolition of property qualifications for public office and for the abolition of the Senate. They have always been concerned with changing and enforcing legislation that affects working people.

Direct political action in support of the Co-operative Commonwealth Federation was taken by the then recently formed Canadian Congress of Labour in 1943 when it endorsed the CCF as "the political Arm of Labour." The Trades and Labour Congress of Canada, the other partner in the founding of the Canadian Labour Congress in 1956, had submitted an annual brief to the federal government as well as maintaining contact with different ministries and the Labour Ministry in particular. The founding of the New Democratic Party was a merger of these two approaches that reflected labour's wish for a more effective means for making its contribution to the political life of Canada.

At the NDP's founding convention in August 1961 it was decided to provide a way for direct affiliation to the NDP of unions, co-operatives and other organizations. This tradition, already established by unions in the United Kingdom that were affiliated to the British Labour Party, now became Canadian practice. Immediately after the founding convention, the trade unions set out to associate their local unions to the NDP. To many of the major unions this meant translating a Statement of Support (S.O.S.) for the party into a financial commitment of five cents per member per month. Most, but not all locals, made this move and about 20 per cent of union locals affiliated, a figure that has remained constant over the years.

Early in the life of the New Party, the trade unions also deliberately decided to remain in the background of the party decision-making processes. While this was the result of some fears expressed by newer members about "union domination," it did not inhibit the CLC from undertaking centralized fundraising for elections, nor did it prevent the Congress from running a Citizenship Month each year to promote legislation for better pensions, housing and social legislation.

Meanwhile, both provincially and nationally, trade unions were given recognition within the party's govern-

ing bodies. This helped in the promotion of direct affiliation by local unions and gave the NDP a solid financial
basis on which to carry out its day-to-day operations.
Slowly but surely the two groups and their membership
gained confidence in each other, a necessary step to
ensure long-term commitments and results.

Following its foundation, the Canadian Labour Congress Political Action Department co-ordinated political
fundraising and the release of union staff for election
purposes. Over the years, many staff personnel from the
CLC, the provincial Federations of Labour and the unions have been assigned to various election roles — from
campaign managers to vote pullers.

But times were changing, and when Prime Minister
Pierre Trudeau, who had fought wage controls during
the previous election, legislated the same controls in
October 1975, the trade union movement realized they
had to confront the government. The CLC Executive
Committee called a meeting of all affiliated unions
where it was decided to hold a national demonstration
against wage controls on Parliament Hill in March of
1976.

The labour movement was never so united! They
came to Ottawa by train, bus and car; one group staged
a walk. The auto workers made a film of their train trip
from Windsor, Ontario. Planes were chartered from
Vancouver and other major cities, and all converged on
the capital. In Hull, the Quebec Federation of Labour
assembled thousands of unionists from across the bridge
to help swell the crowd on the Hill, which was said to be
close to 15 000 persons.

As the CLC approached its biennial convention, the
government showed no signs of weakening its stance, so
the 2300 delegates adopted a plan to hold a "Day of
Protest" in October. The aim of the Congress was to

expand the number of participants by asking the unorganized, pensioners, students and the unemployed — all
victims of the government's policies — to join with
them. The strategy was to hold demonstrations and other
forms of protest in every industrial city and other areas
across the country. Officers and members of the Excu-
tive Council were scheduled to make the same speech in
each of these strategic areas. A centrally directed committee developed and organized the strategy.

Across Canada on October 14, 1976, many thousands
of union members left their workplaces to join in locally
organized Labour Council demonstrations. These varied
in content as they reflected the imagination, region and
culture of Canadians. The key to the success or failure
of all these demonstrations of solidarity was the District
Labour Councils. And successful they were, as over one
million Canadians hit the streets to show their disdain
for the Liberal government and its wage controls. Every
region of Canada played its part, as the following statistics will confirm:*

- Newfoundland 18 000
- Nova Scotia 30 000
- New Brunswick 27 000
- Prince Edward Island 1000
- Quebec 230 000
- Ontario 450 100
- Manitoba 30 800
- Alberta 48 000
- Saskatchewan 27 800
- British Columbia 18 000+

* Figures have been rounded off.
+ The Yukon and Northwest Territories did not have Federations
  of Labour in 1976.

These events were significant in the history of trade union involvement in politics, and were the forerunner of the issue-oriented campaigns to come. They showed how important it was for the labour movement to build bridges to other groups in society, and resulted in effective coalition-building, particularly between elections. They also showed that there was a need to establish funds that would allow the central labour body and its affiliated labour councils adequate finances to make their issue-oriented campaigns more successful.

An even larger demonstration on Parliament Hill was to follow. Building upon these earlier coalitions between the trade unions and like-minded people on an issue-by-issue basis proved its worth when over a hundred thousand people protested the Liberal government's high interest rate policy in 1981. Police and organizers agreed that it was the biggest demonstration ever held in Ottawa. A few years later, when the newly elected Progressive Conservative government attempted to de-index the old age pension, a similar coalition of groups from across the country was successful in convincing the government to forgo its budget proposal — although the Tories have since found another way of accomplishing their objective.

These types of political action, along with the four-year fight to defeat the Free Trade deal with the United States and the struggle against transport deregulation, privatization of government agencies and Crown corporations, VIA Rail cuts, and the GST, have proved to be an effective way of supporting and building the NDP. Working side by side in all these campaigns, the unions and the party have reached a high level of consultation. Trade unions are represented at every level of the party's governing bodies. A unique arrangement, found nowhere else in the industrial world, allows the political action director of the Congress to sit at the weekly caucus meeting of the federal NDP members.

The 1984 CLC convention passed a resolution requiring each affiliate to pay five cents per member per month to a social fund that soon became known as "the Nickel Fund." The Labour Councils now receive funding to help them in their local campaigns. These two decisions have added more financial muscle to single-issue campaigning.

Between and during election campaigns, direct party support is encouraged by an organized approach to local union members through on-the-job canvasses and telephone banks. Workers are approached in the workplace by fellow members who are usually part of the Political Action Committee or by an executive of their union. When party supporters are identified their names are turned over to the campaign committee. Many later become active in both the NDP and the election campaign. Telephone banks have become an integral part of successful electioneering. While leaflets are still used, particularly for educational purposes, modern-day trade union election activities have been honed to a fine point and are recognized as an important part of the party's election machinery.

As Stanley Knowles noted in his 1961 book, the founding of the New Democratic Party was not a "beginning, it was a culmination." All the work and efforts to build the party since have shown that the two major organizations in the founding of the New Party have forged a solid partnership. This can only bode well for its future success.

The Yukon

Max Fraser and Tony Penikett

The last two decades have seen a big change in the Yukon's economy, population and politics. These changes have been marked by the decline of the Conservative party and the rise of the NDP.

There is an early socialist tradition in the territory, however. The Yukon was conscious of worldwide labour/socialist activism at the turn of the century and was, for a while, part of it. Socialists agitated for rights for workers, women and natives; they sought "home rule" in Canada's northern colony. But as elsewhere, this movement was ahead of its time. It was not until the 1980s that a coalition of workers, women, natives and environmentalists elected the first social democratic government in Canada's "top left-hand corner."

In the early 1900s there were not one but two socialist parties in the Yukon's capital, Dawson City. "The Yukon Legislative Labour Association" was dedicated to improving the lot of workers and, in this northern colony of Canada, achieving "home rule" for Yukoners. Sadly, no YLLA members were elected to the Yukon Territorial Council, but two Liberals who associated with the group throughout its lecture series in the winter of 1908–9 were elected in the 1909 council elections, the first wholly elected council. A group called the Dawson Socialist

Party emerged from the YLLA but there is little record of their activity.

There is no evidence of socialist electoral activity in the territory through the First World War–Depression era, but the sun shone again during Second World War when a group of Mine Mill union activists in Dawson City invited the CCF in Vancouver to send a representative to speak to their group. Arthur J. Turner wrote about his eight-week trip through the north in his book, *Somewhere — A Perfect Place*. Turner toured the goldfields, holding meetings, distributing literature and signing up CCF members. According to Dawson resident and CCF Club founder Art Fry, people in the union local at the Yukon Consolidated Gold Corporation (YCGC) "didn't know the difference between the CCF and the Communists, so we passed a motion to send out for an organizer of the CCF" and put up $400 to cover costs. He explains that at the time, "Stalin and the Communists were in the dog-house" because of the non-aggression pact between the Soviet Union and Germany, and the communist Labour Progressive Party was under wartime controls. "So we had a communist union and a social democratic political arm," says Fry.

The CCF elected one member to the Territorial Council, Alex Smith, who represented Whitehorse from 1944 to 1947. No CCF candidates ran in 1947, but in 1949 the CCF candidate in Dawson, Charles J. "Bunny" Lelievre was elected for a three-year term. According to Art Fry, Lelievre introduced in the Yukon much of the progressive legislation pioneered by the new CCF government in Saskatchewan and succeeded in getting much of it passed. CCFer Mike Comadain later became mayor of Dawson.

Out to win the federal seat for the Yukon in 1945, the CCF was thwarted by a Labour Progressive Party candidate from B.C. who came north to spoil their chances. (The Conservative won.) By the time of the 1949 federal election, the Yukon seat had been re-arranged by Ottawa to include the Mackenzie district of the Northwest Territories. CCF candidate James E. Stephens, from Yellowknife, ran a distant third against independent Matt Berry, also from Yellowknife, and Liberal Aubrey Simmons of Whitehorse, who won.

A decline in the Yukon economy in the fifties was accompanied by a decline in CCF activity. No CCF candidate ran in the federal elections of 1953, 1957 or 1958 in the Yukon, and no one carried the banner for the "New Party" in 1962, 1963 or 1965. In 1968, Steelworkers rep Robert McLaren was on the ballot for the NDP, getting 5 percent of the vote. Things were better for his successor in both the job and the candidacy; Harvey Kent received 12 percent of Yukon votes in 1972. Now we were getting somewhere.

The 1960s and '70s were a time of development for the Yukon. New mines, roads and power projects were started. With the growth in population and industry came greater labour activity and interest in alternatives to the traditional Conservative-Liberal rivalry in the North. There was a new awareness in favour of native rights, women's rights and the environment. Communications between the Yukon and southern Canada improved and people found themselves more in touch with national trends.

At the time, Yukon politics consisted mainly of the Conservatives and Liberals fighting for control of the Whitehorse Chamber of Commerce and the city council, in the chamber itself, and as members of the Territorial Council. Natives, workers, women and environmentalists did not count. The Territorial Council was not taken seriously; it was the butt of a lot of local jokes. Disputes were routinely taken to the Minister of Northern Affairs in Ottawa for resolution — he had the real power in the Yukon.

The growing popularity of the New Democratic Party in western Canada made an impression on Yukon people who were looking for a progressive alternative to the old parties. The "corporate welfare bum" federal election of 1972 saw Wally Firth become the first ever NDP MP from north of the 60th parallel. (The person who was to become the Yukon's first NDP premier, Tony Penikett, travelled from the Yukon to manage Firth's campaign.) Meanwhile, Yukoners looked "Outside" and saw provincial NDP governments in B.C., Manitoba and Saskatchewan, and the party holding the balance of power in Ottawa.

Suddenly the idea of changing things seemed possible.

In 1973, forty-three delegates met in Whitehorse to form a territorial (provincial) section of the party. In 1974, a federal convention accepted their bid for equal status with other provincial sections. As federal candidate in the 1974 federal election, Penikett got a sobering 20 percent of the vote — up from 12 percent two years before. It was a big gain, but it showed how much farther the party had to go.

Two out of three NDP candidates were elected in the territorial election in the fall of 1974: Fred Berger in Dawson and Stu McCall in Faro won their seats, but Penikett, in downtown Whitehorse, did not. The pair sat in what was still a colonial form of council, with executive powers mostly in the hands of Ottawa-appointed civil servants. The local Liberals ran a slate of candidates, electing none. Conservatives ran as independents, saying the time for party politics at the territorial level was not at hand. They would wait until 1978, when the legislature was enlarged from twelve to sixteen seats.

Operating in this undisciplined body proved difficult for the NDP. There were no Opposition and Government sides to the House. Berger had no special status in the House even though he was a party leader; and there was no research or support staff to help MLAs do their work. The next time they went to the polls, both Berger and McCall were defeated.

The party fielded candidates in fourteen of sixteen ridings in 1978, and this time Penikett, now a Whitehorse city councillor, was successful. He won by a small margin in a five-way race. Trouble was, he was the only New Democrat, now on the Opposition bench with two independents and two Liberals, who took status as Official Opposition. This legislature inherited important new responsibilities. In 1979, Joe Clark's Conservative government in Ottawa granted the Yukon responsible government when they instructed the commissioner to follow the advice of elected members sitting in cabinet.

The 1979 and 1980 federal campaigns boosted the party profile in the Yukon and strengthened the organization. The NDP reached twenty-five and twenty percent of the popular vote with native activist Joe Jack (1979) and labour rep Jim McCullough (1980) as candidates, both placing third behind the Liberals and Tory MP Erik Nielsen.

The year 1981 marked a turning point for the party in the Yukon. After three years of lonely battle in the legislature, Penikett got some company. Maurice Byblow, the teacher from Faro who ran as an independent and defeated NDP MLA Stu McCall in 1978, announced in September that he would join the party and sit with Penikett in the House. A by-election victory by former judge Roger Kimmerly in October 1981 gave the party three seats to two for the Liberals and one remaining independent. The NDP were now the Official Opposition.

This was the perfect springboard for the Yukon general election of June 7, 1982. The NDP came out of it with six MLAs to the Tories' ten. They were still the government, but the lines were drawn with the Liberals and independents gone. Penikett, Byblow and Kimmerly were all re-elected in their ridings. They were joined by Piers McDonald, a trade unionist from Elsa (Mayo riding); Margaret Joe, native activist in Whitehorse North Centre; and Dave Porter, native activist in the rural riding of Campbell.

The 1984 federal election was uneventful. Erik Nielsen got his biggest vote ever in the national Tory sweep. The NDP ran third with unionist Sybil Frei garnering 16 percent of the vote.

An arrogant Tory government in Whitehorse set itself up for defeat between 1982 and 1985; even a change in leadership didn't help. In the spring of 1985, Yukoners elected their first New Democrat government: eight NDP MLAs, six PCs and two Liberals. It added up to an NDP minority. Five of our six from the previous term were re-elected, though one took the honours in a different riding: Dave Porter went from Campbell to his home riding of Watson Lake, where three Tory candidates split the vote to let him win by nine votes. In Campbell riding, Sam Johnston, former chief of the Teslin Tlingit Indian Band for thirteen years, held the NDP seat. Faro, however, where Maurice Byblow did not seek re-election for family reasons, went to the Liberals. But in Klondike, City Councillor Art Webster took the seat on his second try. In Old Crow, the tiny, isolated community north of the Arctic Circle, another native activist, Norma Kassi, won by six votes in a two-way race.

In total, fifteen votes made the difference in two ridings and helped form an NDP government. Of the new caucus of eight, five members were rural and four were native. Margaret Joe became the first native woman cabinet minister in Canada, and Sam Johnson was elected as the first native Speaker of a legislative assembly in the country. Two years later, a by-election in the rural riding of Tatchun was forced by the resignation of the Liberal leader. The new government's appeal to rural and native voters was confirmed when popular local candidate Danny Joe, former chief of the Selkirk Indian Band, took the riding easily in February 1987. Now the party had a solid majority to work with.

About this time, federal MP Erik Nielsen announced his resignation. Audrey McLaughlin narrowly won a tough NDP nomination contest and the right to stand as the candidate in a federal by-election. In July 1987 she took the seat by 300 votes over the mayor of Whitehorse, a right-wing Liberal. Yukoners liked her style: in November 1988 Audrey was re-elected in the general election with more than 50 percent of the vote.

Just months later, Penikett called his first general election — for February 20, 1989. It was a cold campaign, but the party came out on top: nine NDP seats to seven for the Tories (with Sam Johnston as Speaker, a working majority of eight votes to seven) and an increased popular vote. Dave Porter left politics and did not seek re-election. His riding was lost by just three votes. Roger Kimmerly left the territory and was replaced by Joyce Hayden as NDP MLA for Whitehorse South Centre. Maurice Byblow was back in politics and the caucus, representing his former seat of Faro.

In the last twenty years, the Yukon's politics have changed radically. At the party's founding convention in

1973, idealism and optimism abounded, but few thought it possible that within just a few years we would be the Official Opposition, and soon after the government. And not even the big dreamers thought it possible to see a New Democrat MP come out of such a conservative place, let alone the national leader of our party.

The reasons for the change in our party's fortunes in the Yukon lie in the change in the Yukon's population. Says Penikett, the territory changed radically, and the NDP more accurately reflected the New Yukon than did the Tories. The Liberals couldn't make up their minds if they were Laurier Liberals or Trudeau Liberals, and some went to the Tories, others chose to come to the NDP.

The Yukon experience is proof that politics is the art of the possible. Credit has to go to those who stood for office, the pioneers and those who have served and are serving, and also to the core of hard-working activists who give up a good part of their lives for a cause they believe in. The secret to our party's success up north has been a dedication to local issues and local traditions, interpreting the democratic socialist vision in our community.

As the Yukon evolves, a shift in power, money and social relations is taking place. What we are seeing is the decolonization of the Yukon Territory, where socialists are in the driver's seat and issues are being settled locally, not in Ottawa. The groups neither heard nor represented at the beginning of the century, nor as little as ten years ago, now have a voice. This coalition of interests — workers, women, natives, environmentalists — is supporting a government that has given them a voice and a role in making decisions about the future of the territory. It's called social democracy.

The Northwest Territories

Cooper Langford

The NDP got its start in the Northwest Territories more than twenty years ago, in meetings held around kitchen tables of like-minded northerners. Pierre Trudeau had won his first election when the party moved north of the 60th parallel. One Liberal in Ottawa represented people scattered over the region that includes about one-third of the Canadian land mass. The Northwest Territories had always been a fairly strong Liberal territory, electing popular representatives like Merv Hardy, who died in office and was replaced by his wife. But in the late 1960s and early 1970s changes were afoot.

"I don't think people were too happy with the incumbent at that time," recalls Wally Firth, an early member of the territorial party who went on to represent the Northwest Territories in Ottawa from 1972 to 1979. "New Democrats had not run a candidate before that time. Some people made a call here and there. That's the way it was done and that's the way we won the election in '72. Just ordinary working people. They paid for their own phone calls and helped here and there. Before you knew it, there it was."

In those early days, the party rallied around the theme "Our Land, Our Man." In the years leading up to the Berger Inquiry on pipeline construction in the Mackenzie Valley — which would focus national attention on the problems of development and native entitlement — settlement of land claims and questioning of pipeline construction were strong planks in the local platform. When the Berger Inquiry was announced in 1974, there was a minority in government in Ottawa, with the NDP holding the balance of power. "I still maintain the Berger Inquiry was part of what we called our shopping list," says Firth. "We were not gung-ho, let's go for it. We were saying, 'Look, if you're going to do something like that, let's have a debate.' We were saying, 'If we're going to look at a way of moving oil and gas, why don't we examine the idea of building a railway instead of a pipeline?'"

One of the other main tasks Firth set for himself in Ottawa was to divide the Northwest Territories into two separate ridings. After having its fill of his "lobbying and lobbying," the Liberal government adopted the idea. Feeling he had accomplished in Ottawa what he had set out to do, Firth decided to leave Parliament at the time of the 1978 elections. He was succeeded by an up-and-coming Dene politician, Georges Erasmus — later president of the Assembly of First Nations.

Erasmus's candidacy generated excitement in the party and brought new members crawling out of the woodwork. Tony Penniket, now the NDP government leader in the Yukon, was sent to organize his campaign out of a decrepit shack in Yellowknife's Old Town, where plumbing consisted of a simple "honey bucket." But the timing of the 1978 election and the perception that Erasmus was a native-affairs, single-issue candidate worked against the campaign.

"Part of the problem was that it was a spring election," says Debbie Delancey, who joined the NDP to help Erasmus's campaign. "A lot of people were in the bush hunting. It wasn't the time to get the vote in the communities." Erasmus was defeated by the Progressive Conservative candidate and left federal politics. Firth jumped back in after the Clark government was defeated in 1979. He lost to the incumbent Conservative by less than twenty votes after a judicial recount.

Meanwhile, the NDP in the eastern Arctic riding of Nunatsiaq had sent the first Inuit MP to Ottawa. Peter Ittinuar, then twenty-nine years old, appeared the perfect candidate for the Inuit. He was fluent in Inuktitut, had studied political science at Carleton University in Ottawa, and had taught the Inuit language at the University of Ottawa. Ittinuar was a strong supporter of dividing the Northwest Territories to create a territory in the east called Nunavut, Inuktitut for "our land." When the Liberals threw their support behind the plan for division in 1982, Ittinuar crossed the floor of the Commons and joined the government. He was unable to regain his seat in 1984 and returned to Rankin Inlet, his home community on the shores of Hudson Bay.

Back in the west, the party faithful were consolidating their position as the party that would champion land claims and native rights. "The party always saw that as a priority and the main selling point for the western Arctic," says Delancey. But party organizers were having trouble drafting a strong native candidate for the 1984 campaign. Bertha Allen, a strong grass-roots territorial political activist who helped the N.W.T. Native Women's Association, agreed to run. Although Allen was a popular individual, she was inexperienced on the big political stage and her campaign was unsuccessful.

On the local scene in the mid-1980s the NDP became embroiled in debate on whether to run candidates for the territorial legislature. Government in the territory operates on a consensus model. There are no political parties. An eight-member executive committee functions like a provincial cabinet. Regular MLAs are both opposition and government insofar as they criticize the executive, debate its legislation and eventually pass legislation. It is a system that has benefits and drawbacks.

At the 1986 convention the question of promoting party politics in the North split the membership. On one hand, delegates argued that consensus government wasn't working. People were electing MLAs without having a strong sense of their platforms. On the other, the proposal's critics claimed that importing the European parliamentary model could prejudice the political and constitutional aspirations of the Dene and Métis people. (At that time, the Dene and Métis wanted to achieve their political aims through guaranteed representation in public government in a western territory.) The issue was so thorny that the convention could only decide to put the matter to further study, issue a report and poll the members' opinions. The study was completed by the spring of 1987 and circulated among party members. A mail-in ballot measured the members' responses. The party voted to stay out of partisan politics by a narrow margin.

But the members in the community of Fort Smith near the Alberta border had other ideas, and ran an NDP candidate in territorial elections in the fall of 1987. That sent the executive scrambling for a line that would not create the impression of division in the ranks. "We publicly said, this is great," says Delancey, who was the local president at the time. "Here are a group of people who believe the party is so great they want to run a candidate. Of course he's not an official candidate. It was all bullshit." The NDP candidate lost to Jeannie Marie-Jewell, a woman who now sits on the territorial executive committee as the Social Services Minister. And the issue of party politics in the Northwest Territories is still alive.

About this time the Nunatsiaq riding association also began agitating for independent status, and more or less achieved that position.

In the run-up to the 1988 election, the NDP searched long and hard for a native candidate to present to the voters. The search was unsuccessful and the nomination went to Wayne Cahill, a union supporter from Fort Smith. Cahill lost to Liberal Ethel Blondin, the first native woman to become a member of Parliament.

Since the 1988 election, the NDP has lost a good deal of its public image. Current executive members estimate that membership stands at around 120 people. Recent conventions have sorely illustrated a rift between labour and non-labour members of the party, which has its roots in disputes from the mid-1980s.

There is much work to be done if the NDP wishes to make a significant gain at the next election.

British Columbia

Alexander B. Macdonald

The hundred-year-old story of the NDP in B.C. begins in strife between labour and the powerful resource extraction companies. Then, as now, the economy depended upon development and sale of its natural resources on the markets of the world. In this mountain province, less than 5 percent of the land can be put to agricultural use.

One hundred years ago, most communities were single-industry company towns. Companies owned the mineral or timber rights. They owned the stores, too, and the workers' homes.

In the Kootenays of the southeast, hard-rock miners and smelter workers formed trade unions. Their unions had to strike to gain recognition and the right to collective bargaining. They struck for living wages and against an appalling accident and death toll in the deep underground shafts. They met bitter resistance from militant employer organizations in the form of arrests, blacklistings, strike-breakers and attacks by armed company security guards. They dared to go on strike at a time when any union activity was deemed a criminal conspiracy by the common law.

The miners' leaders were equally militant. Leadership came from revolutionary Wobblies drifting north from the industrial worksites of the American West, and from immigrants with a tradition of job action and socialism formed in the "dark satanic mills" of industrial Britain. These leaders understood that unions could only do so much without political action.

The labour movement spread at the turn of the century to the coal seams of Vancouver Island, to the isolated logging camps, to salmon canneries and flour mills. Soon, labour formed its own Socialist Party of Canada and ran candidates for the provincial legislature, an assembly that in those days was dominated by representatives of the resource companies. These representatives wanted immigrant labour from the Orient to work long hours for low wages. They sought laws to combat trade unionism. And above all, they sought lucrative mineral rights, timber licences, land grants, and utility and railway franchises for the companies. In the pursuit of this program, politicians were bought and sold. An enduring corruption penetrated the politics of British Columbia.

Labour and capital joined issue in the legislature with the election in 1903 of two Socialists, both from the coal-mining communities near Nanaimo on Vancouver Island. One, J. W. Hawthornthwaite, rose to shock the comfortable company members of that assembly with a ringing declaration: "Mr. Speaker: I stand for nothing less than an end to the exploitation of human labour by a master class." For such revolutionary socialism Hawthornthwaite and his colleague, Parker Williams, were derided as "impossibilists." But the two were also "possibilists" in the pursuit of immediate reforms. They were able to wrest lasting gains because in the unstable politics of the times, the province's premiers had to flirt with socialists to hold office.

Thus, before the Great War, these forerunners of the NDP won union rights under a Trade Unions Act. The eight-hour day made its appearance, at first only for miners in the underground shafts. Some safety measures were won, and later the establishment of a Workers' Compensation Board. And the Socialists fought for laws to protect farmers and orchardists, which eventually led to marketing boards. But the long years until 1929 were not favourable to further labour-socialist advance. Through those years, the labour cause won no more than 13 percent of the vote and elected no more than four members to any legislature.

When war came in 1914, nothing mattered but the fight for King and Country. Then in 1919, the crushing of the Winnipeg General Strike spread despair to the Far West. Also in 1919, following the lead of the Russian Revolution, many left the movement to form the Communist Party. Indeed, in the prosperous twenties, growing disenchantment with that revolution hurt the socialist cause. By 1925, under the banner of the Independent Labour Party, membership had fallen to 147, scattered through only ten branches. But few as they were they kept the flame alive.

The canniest was Angus MacInnis. He was a Vancouver streetcar driver who had the wit to marry Grace Woodsworth, the daughter of J. S. Woodsworth. Angus became a trade union leader, a school trustee, an alderman, and in 1935, a member of the Parliament of Canada. He won the trust of the voters without ever hiding his socialist goals. He campaigned on issues such as old age security, as incremental steps toward these goals. His election successes, along with his tact and patience, moderated the passionate thoeretical disputes that threatened to tear the movement apart. "Theory," he would say, "bakes no scones."

The onset of the Great Depression made 1929 the watershed year in B.C. politics. The province was on its way to polarization. Elections came to be a choice between two sides — on the one side, those who broadly supported politics and economics as usual, and on the other, their opponents who insisted that people's needs must come first. By 1933, while hungry men greased the rails to stop trains and ride boxcars in search of work, the CCF was founded and thousands flocked to join. They questioned the sanity of poverty in the midst of potential abundance, as the NDPers do today. In the provincial election of 1933, seven CCFers became members of the legislature, and the new party won 31.5 percent of the vote. In 1934, a party task-force led by the charismatic Dr. Lyle Telford toured the province. The number of CCF clubs rose to 185.

But government was to elude the CCF. There was internal division within the new party. Revolutionary socialists fought for power against moderates, with personal ambitions often cloaked in ideological righteousness. The House leader chosen in 1933 was an Anglican minister and Victorian gentleman, Robert Connell, a moderate who refused to be bound by the decisions of a party convention controlled by the far left. In August of 1936, the provincial executive formally expelled the House leader from the party.

Meanwhile, the old parties and their press were eagerly seizing upon the inflammatory statements of a few CCFers. They denounced the CCF for having a program "that might be imposed by machine guns in Papua." CCFers (and some had said it) "preferred Karl Marx to Jesus Christ." They looked forward to "red funerals." They stood for "companionate marriage." They would "give votes to Chinamen."

But for the able, dedicated leadership in the party and legislature, the CCF would have foundered. CCF members of the provincial legislature were making their cause a full-time job, on a legislative allowance of $1600 a year, including all expenses. The Winches, father and son, were on relief when they were elected in 1933. With fellow MLAs Grace MacInnis, Grant MacNeil, Gretchen Steeves, Colin Cameron and Arthur Turner, they tirelessly spread the gospel in the legislature and at the worksites. Some were arrested on the picket line at a cannery strike at Blubber Bay. During the occupation of the Vancouver post office by hungry men from the relief camps, Harold Winch, then party leader, was beaten with police billy clubs.

In halls, on the radio and in the legislature, CCFers tirelessly spread the message of their socialist goals: social ownership of large financial and other institutions upon which the life of communities depended, and "production for use and not for profit," a phrase strangely old-fashioned but curiously relevant today. At the same time, CCFers worked for immediate social reforms in education, working conditions and health care. Through public education and persuasion, they made a provincial medical plan a political issue that in time became a reality.

By 1941, the CCF had achieved internal unity. It grew in popularity in the Second World War years as more people said no to a social order of depression and war. This caused frightened Liberals and Conservatives to form a coalition for their political salvation. Elections became two-party contests in every constituency. Against coalition candidates in the 1945 election, the CCF, although the strongest of the parties with 38 percent of the vote, was only able to win ten seats. By 1949, the coalition was surviving only by stealing planks from the CCF platform.

The coalition broke up in 1950, torn by rivalries over the spoils of office. This time the two parties decided they could beat the CCF through the device of a "preferential ballot." Voters would mark their ballots for a choice of candidates in the order of their preferences. Liberals were confidently expecting their voters to give the second choice to Free Enterprise Conservatives, and Conservatives to return the favour. In fact, in 1952 both old parties were hoist on their own petard. A revitalized evangelical Social Credit movement garnered most of the second choices and won government with one seat more than the CCF.

Social Credit quickly became the new coalition of the right. It was a formidable political force under Premier W. A. C. Bennett. Quietly he awarded lavish resource rights to foreign corporate friends and cashed in on their political contributions. Loudly he denounced the CCF as the dupes of "labour bosses" and of Moscow. And with the coming of prosperous times he built power dams and black-topped highways.

In the fifties, the CCF under Arnold Webster, a Christian Socialist, and later Bob Strachan, a Scottish carpenter, struggled to survive and rebuild. And struggled, too, with some success, to wring from government some of the housing and human welfare reforms that are part of a modern welfare state. Because of CCF pressure, Bennett also socialized the B.C. Ferries and extended service to scattered communities up the long coastline.

The CCF had its last valiant hurrah in 1960. Calling for public ownership of the generation and distribution of electricity, the CCF created the election issue and was on its way to victory. But there was a last-minute socialist scare. On election day, a black headline in the Vancouver *Province* read: "A CCF victory will cost the province 10,000 jobs."

Losing government, the CCF nevertheless won its issue. In 1963, Bennett brought the B.C. Electric Company under public ownership.

In 1961, the CCF became the NDP. Stronger labour ties brought better funding and poll-by-poll organization in the constituencies. Issues changed as more emphasis was put on the quality of life, protection of the environment, the opening of the forests to recreational use, regional planning to avert the worst effects of urban sprawl, and civil, labour and human rights. Fresh recruits were attracted to the ranks. But government still eluded the NDP. Then, in a feisty campaign in 1972 Dave Barrett led the NDP to victory. Dave was east-side Vancouver-born, and thrice blessed at birth. Both of his parents were socialists, and they begat in him, along with other gifts, a sense of humour.

In its three and a half years of government, the NDP took the cork out of the bottle. It passed a record three hundred pieces of progressive legislation. Highlights included:

- an agricultural land reserve to preserve scarce arable land for food production for generations to come
- a publicly owned timber conglomerate
- public auto and general insurance
- socialization of the marketing and export of natural gas, with returns to the public treasury of more than $1 billion
- locally elected community human resource boards, with block funding, to allot health and social services in accordance with community needs
- the first native Indian school districts in Canada
- the first legal aid plan to make assistance a right, not a charity; Pharmacare, Denticare, public-sector bargaining rights, a Human Rights Board outlaw-

ing acts of discrimination, and a start on the road toward pay equity for women.

But, again, there was a coalition of the right. Three Liberal MLAs and the only Conservative struck their colours to join the Social Credit under Bill Bennett. The strengthened Social Credit beat the NDP at the end of 1975, even though the NDP received more votes than it had in 1972. Some said the NDP government had done too much too quickly. But never had people been so publicly aware or participated more in the politics of the province.

Premier Bill Bennett at once applied the tar brush to the NDP record. To "prove" that the NDP government had been "shovelling money out of the back of a truck," he brought in outside chartered accountants. They reported a deficit of $350 million. They did not report that Bennett had paid bills that had not yet fallen due, and even sent an unneeded $175 million to the insurance corporation that was promptly returned when the accountants had finished their work. In fact, Finance Minister Dave Stupich had left no deficit. And the capital assets of the province had doubled during the NDP term in government.

Bob Skelly succeeded Dave Barrett as leader of the Opposition. A terrier Opposition fought to maintain the gains won in government. Many were saved, including the agricultural land reserves and the Autoplan (although General Insurance was sold off). Among the losses were the community resource boards and the Petroleum Corporation.

Since 1975 the NDP, although winning about 45 percent of the votes, has not defeated the new coalition. The Conservative counter-revolution has begun: cutbacks of government services; fiscal restraint; hurting those in need; privatization; deregulation. The greed ethics of the times have been sold as virtues: "Unemployment insurance creates unemployment." "Welfare for single mothers creates single mothers!"

Two strands have wended their way through the first hundred years of the NDP story in B.C. and will go on for years to come. The first is a basic political issue: the management of natural resources. On the one side are the forces that want to exploit these resources on terms most favourable to the balance sheets of large international corporations. On the other side are those who want the development, processing and sale of these resources with the best returns to the people of the province and with the best protection of the natural heritage. The second is a basic tension within the NDP. On the one side are those stressing the need for immediate reforms and on the other those whose main stress is on the need for a new social order. Neither is exclusive of the other.

Alberta

Alvin Finkel

Until recently, Alberta has seemed an electoral waste-land for social democrats. But an examination of the historical record suggests that the province's citizens have not always been as conservative as some think. Indeed, the CCF's failure to take off in Alberta may have been more the result of organizational mistakes than infertile ideological ground.

The CCF was formed in Calgary in 1932 at a meeting of left-wing organizations called together by the Ginger Group of MPs, the majority of whom were United Farmers of Alberta representatives. It is debatable whether the decision to simply affiliate existing parties and movements to the CCF helped the new party, though grass-roots organization proved disastrous. The UFA and the Canadian Labour Party, the major groups from Alberta that affiliated with the CCF, were models of disunity and increasingly out of touch with their electoral base.

The UFA was a particularly confusing phenomenon. Formed initially as a lobbying organization for farm interests, the UFA had entered the electoral battle in the provincial and federal elections of 1921. It formed the provincial government in 1921 and was re-elected in 1926 and 1930. Its members in the 1920s had focused on grass-roots democracy and in the 1930s on public ownership of resources, banks and industry. But the UFA government of the 1920s behaved much like any other government, stressing cabinet and caucus solidarity rather than constituency input. In the 1930s, the UFA government, ignoring its members' annual convention resolutions, concentrated on fiscal prudence. The result was that while the UFA organization was calling for society to be turned upside down, the UFA government was struggling to uphold the *status quo*. For voters, it was the government and not the party membership who represented the UFA, and the UFA-CCF label, which the members proudly adopted, proved a millstone for the new party.

Somewhat similarly, the CLP, having adopted a strategy in the 1920s of working closely with the UFA, was unable to escape the taint of the government's conservative record in the early thirties. Farm foreclosures, inadequate relief, poorly enforced labour legislation: all were laid at the door of the new CCF because it had chosen to work with established groups rather than establish its own grass-roots organization to press its demands for social ownership and social justice.

The Social Credit movement of William Aberhart, the charismatic radio preacher, made no such error. Aberhart's "social credit clubs," formed from 1932 onwards, dotted the province and created a political force that smothered both the UFA and the CLP in the provincial and federal elections of 1935. Aberhart promised to issue social dividends of twenty-five dollars per month to every adult Albertan if he became premier, and to fix prices of goods. He did not deliver but he was able to blame the federal government, which unsurprisingly failed to give up its control over currency and banks to allow Aberhart to force the financial institutions to cough up the money required for the province to issue social dividends.

Social Credit's broken promises might have created opportunities for a rival left-of-centre party (although Social Credit later became demonstrably right-wing, it had a left-wing aura in its early years and was reviled as "socialist" by the daily press and business organizations) but the CCF was still paralysed by its association with the UFA and CLP. The UFA did not abandon direct involvement in politics until 1939 and the CLP only wound up its affairs in 1942.

Though hampered by the continued operation of these two parties, a few CCF activists began in the late thirties to assemble CCF clubs across the province. Elmer Roper, a printer and long-time labour activist, was a catalyst. Roper edited *Alberta Labour News*, the official organ of the Alberta Federation of Labour from 1921 to 1935 — but in most respects a mouthpiece for Roper's democratic socialist views. In 1935, Roper, who published the *News* as well, changed its name to *People's Weekly*, invited defeated UFA MP William Irvine to become co-editor, and turned the paper into a *de facto* house organ for the CCF.

On Roper's urging, the provincial board of the CCF hired Irvine and Henry Spencer, another MP who had fallen before the Social Credit onslaught in 1935, as party organizers. Both men had been advocates in the 1920s of the "social credit" doctrines of Major C. H. Douglas. Now, having decided that monetary inflation alone would not resolve the problems of capitalism, the two men sought to persuade Albertans of the need for a more thoroughgoing restructuring of economic and social institutions.

The CCF's new-found respect among progressive voters first showed in an Edmonton-wide provincial by-election in April 1942. Elmer Roper was a surprise winner. Over the next two and a half years, party membership soared from 2500 to 12 000. Indeed, by the time of the August 1944 provincial election, the CCF could boast 4000 more paid-up members than the governing party. The 1944 provincial election, however, proved a disappointment to the CCF. Its share of the popular vote was respectable: just under 25 percent. But that support was thinly scattered and translated into only two seats in the fifty-five-seat legislature. Roper, who became party leader in 1942, was re-elected in Edmonton and was joined in the legislature by Aylmer Liesemer, a Calgary school teacher.

The rise of the CCF and the move of Social Credit to the right had caused the business community to remove its support from the anti-Socred coalition and to put monies into the Social Credit campaign. Under the leadership of Ernest Manning, who inherited Aberhart's mantle upon his death in 1943, Social Credit became the darling of big business in Alberta. Its anti-labour legislation in the late forties, its denunciations of universal social programs and its *laisser-faire* attitude towards the oil and gas industries that took off after the war endeared the Socreds to the rich.

The failure to win more seats produced a sense of defeatism in the CCF. The 1944 campaign had also created internal ideological divisions. Unlike the Saskatchewan CCF, which had stressed welfare measures in its successful provincial campaign that year, the Alberta CCF had focused on provincial ownership of resource industries and utilities. Left-wingers in the party, including provincial secretary William Irvine, even favoured an electoral pact with the Labour Progressive Party (the renamed Communists), noting that the transferable ballot system in Alberta made it possible for parties to run against one another but establish agreements to encourage supporters to mark their seconds for the rival left-wing party. The national CCF, unwilling to accept a local arrangement of this kind, prevented its consummation. It would have enraged CCF unionists in Ontario and British Columbia who were bitter rivals of the communists for control of various unions. So the CCF and the communists who, by working together, would have elected five CCFers and one LPPer, ended up attacking one another as they attacked Social Credit. But association with the communists on any level would have been highly compromising and opposed to labour's fundamental interests.

Throughout the 1950s, party left-wingers and moderates clashed, with the latter accusing the former of wrecking the party's electoral chances and the left-wingers charging their opponents with opportunism. In practice, the province's considerable oil wealth in the period after the Imperial strike near Leduc in February 1947 gave a considerable advantage to the party in power. Though its overall rhetoric and its record in many ways were reactionary, the Manning party had the funds available to pave highways and build hospitals in election years at a dizzying pace.

A small group kept the party alive. Roper remained leader until 1955, retiring from the position only after having lost his legislative seat. The CCF never held more than two seats in the legislature and its share of the popular vote lost a half-life at each provincial election, until in 1959 it won only 4 percent of the vote and lost both rural east-central Alberta seats it had won in 1955. Apart from Roper, key party stalwarts included Irvine; Floyd Johnson, Roper's successor as leader; and Nellie Peterson. Peterson was one of only a small group of women in leadership positions in a male-dominated party. A farmer and daughter of UFA activists, Peterson's commitment to a socialist transformation of society led her to beat the backwoods in search of members for the new party as it formed in the 1930s. By 1944 she was one of two provincial organizers for the party and later she served for thirteen years as provincial secretary. Though privately she left little doubt that the party's chances of electoral success were slim, she soldiered on in the belief that each generation of socialists must keep a flame burning, however small, to pass on to the next generation.

Peterson, Irvine and their associates spent much of their time in the fifties researching and propagandizing on international issues. They wanted to expose the Cold War as an artificial creation of reactionary American interests. Such views were anathema to Roper, who wanted the party to become more mainstream. But the majority remained idealistic and, when first presented with the idea of a new labour-based party, they rejected it on the grounds that non-socialists would be active in it and would weaken the socialist thrust that in the tiny Alberta CCF, at least, remained predominant.

When the provincial NDP was created in 1962, the hard-headed labour leaders at its forefront made every effort to marginalize the old CCFers and to project a more moderate social democratic image. Neil Reimer, chief Alberta representative of the Oil, Chemical and Atomic Workers, became the party's first leader in 1963.

Electoral success, however, came slowly to the NDP. The first victory came in October 1966, when Pincher Creek–Crowsnest, a rural southern Alberta seat with a large representation of active and retired miners, elected Garth Turcott in a by-election. Turcott subsequently exposed in the legislature questionable private dealings by two cabinet ministers. A commission appointed by Manning claimed the two had broken no laws, although they were guilty of enriching themselves privately while holding public office. Reimer's strident campaign in the 1967 provincial election against the highhandedness and apparent corruption of the Socreds struck a chord with voters. But the chief beneficiaries were the Progressive Conservatives led by Peter Lougheed. With leaders and members younger and more urban than the Socreds, they came to power in 1971.

The NDP, left without a seat in 1967, managed to squeak through a win in Spirit River–Fairview in the Peace country in 1971. The man elected was Grant Notley, a school teacher who became party leader in 1968. Notley had spent ten months organizing the constituency and the electoral triumph was largely a personal one rather than a partisan victory. In the legislature Notley was widely regarded as the most articulate opposition voice. A tireless leader, he worked to build party membership throughout the province during a period when the "energy boom" spread prosperity, however unevenly, and created little space for the left.

Notley, like Reimer, rejected the old CCFers' emphasis on nationalization of industries and focused his critique of the Conservatives on their social, labour and environmental records, all of which reflected pro-corporate bias. But in 1975 and 1979 he remained the only NDPer in the legislature.

The recession that began in 1982 created more demands for interventionism but wily Peter Lougheed, by calling an early election, forestalled a deep erosion of government strength. In the November 1982 election, however, the NDP added one Edmonton seat — Ray Martin in Norwood. After Notley died tragically in a plane crash in October 1984, Martin was elected party leader.

By the time of the 1986 election, the Tories had a new leader, Don Getty, and were viewed by an increasing proportion of the electorate as callous in the face of the growing poverty that was visible in the long lines at the food banks. Labour legislation that temporarily paralysed the construction workers' unions added that group of workers to the already alienated government workers (who had lost the right to strike in 1977) and allowed the NDP, which had won 32 percent of Edmonton's vote in 1982, to win 43 percent of that vote in 1986 and, more significantly, twelve seats in the metropolitan region. Two Calgary seats, two rural seats and 29 percent of the provincial vote suggested that, at long last, social democrats in Alberta, now the Official Opposition, were a potential provincial government.

Party membership, which had rarely exceeded 5000 in the 1970s, reached 20 000 after the 1986 election. The party also managed to elect its first-ever MP from Alberta, Ross Harvey, in Edmonton East in 1988. But the party's failure to elect more MPs and its relatively modest share of the Alberta vote (15 percent) suggested that the NDP (or NDs, as the party leadership now usually referred to themselves) had a tenuous hold on voters. Nonetheless, in the 1989 provincial election, the NDs won sixteen seats once again, losing three of their 1986 seats but picking up three others.

In the legislature, the ND caucus gave voice to the growing feminist and environmental movements in the province as well as to its traditional trade union constituency. The NDs focused on social justice, poverty and the environment, and condemned the Tories for making a fetish of uncontrolled economic development and allowing hospitals, schools and universities to languish under budget cuts while a variety of corporations received subsidies and loans from the government, often without creating or preserving jobs.

Saskatchewan

Georgina M. Taylor

The Saskatchewan CCF-NDP, the most successful of the provincial sections, grew out of a long tradition of reform dating back to the turn of the century. The CCF spirit of rebellious practical idealism was rooted in the farm movement. It was this spirit that was to bring the first democratic socialist government ever elected in Canada to power in 1944 and to lay the foundation for an enduring tradition of socialism in a province which is, to this day, passionately political.

The Saskatchewan farm movement began when discontented farmers organized the Territorial Grain Growers' Association (TGGA) in 1902 to fight the entrenched interests of the grain trade and the railways. Farm people could not get a "square deal" in spite of their near-endless toil. Changing their name to the Saskatchewan Grain Growers' Association (SGGA) when the province came into being, these organized farmers were influential, encouraging in many Saskatchewan people the on-going spirit of co-operation that had begun in the pioneer period. In 1914 the women of the SGGA formed a women's section with the women as full members of the SGGA and the Women Grain Growers (WGG). With agrarian feminist Violet McNaughton as their president, the WGG led the successful suffrage battle which won women the vote and pushed for numerous reforms such as the establishment of the Union Hospital and Municipal Doctor schemes to help improve medical services in the pioneer province.

In 1921 a left-wing group broke with the SGGA, which was dominated by leaders who worked closely with the governing provincial Liberals, to form the Farmers' Union (FU). In 1922 an SGGA "Ginger Group" succeeded in ousting the old guard and began to heal the wounds. So effective was the hold of the Liberals on the province, however, that Saskatchewan did not elect a government of Progressives, the first "third party" in Canada to challenge successfully the two old-line parties. The FU and the SGGA established the Saskatchewan Wheat Pool, which became the most powerful producers' co-operative in Canada. In 1926 the FU and SGGA amalgamated to form the United Farmers of Canada, Saskatchewan Section (UFC), from which the CCF grew.

In 1931 Saskatchewan lay in the iron grip of drought and economic depression. A small delegation, representing the eighty farm and twenty labour leaders who had "marched on Regina," met with the Conservative-dominated provincial cabinet. Premier Anderson did not bother to attend and one cabinet minister lounged with his feet on the table. Another cabinet minister sarcastically told the farmers to stop asking for relief, to go home, plant a garden and milk a cow. Louise Lucas, an assertive farm woman, rose to her feet. Knowing the fundamentals of agriculture, she replied in a clear orator's voice, "Will you kindly tell me how you are going to get milk out of one end when you cannot put hay and water in the other?" Here was the rebellious practical humour and idealism that the largely agrarian people of Saskatchewan loved and respected.

Not having impressed the Cabinet with the gravity of the situation, the twenty members of the small British-style Independent Labour Party (ILP) and eighty representatives of the UFC spent the rest of the day in Regina, planning their next move. The farm people returned to their districts to delight their neighbours with Louise Lucas's wry comment. It spread like a prairie fire.

The Regina marchers were able to convince the grass-roots members of the UFC that the time was right to form a political party. In 1932 the UFC and the ILP joined together to form the Farmer Labour Group. It attended the Calgary Convention to organize the national Co-operative Commonwealth Federation (CCF) and the founding convention in Regina in 1933 to adopt the radical Regina Manifesto as its platform. Retaining the familiar name until after the 1934 provincial election, the Farmer–Labour Party elected five MLAs, "the Quints." M. J. Coldwell, the Regina school teacher who had emigrated from England and was the leader of the ILP, and George Williams of the UFC jockeyed for the leadership of the new party. The leading members of the Saskatchewan party met in Saskatoon to settle the feud. The brilliant Sophia Dixon, who filled the position of Woman President of the UFC and was a member of the CCF provincial and federal councils, recalls a day of bitter wrangling between two men who were "acting like two little boys fighting in a playground." Williams had just been elected an MLA so it was agreed that he would be the leader of the provincial party and they would throw their efforts behind getting Coldwell elected as MP for Rosetown so that he could carry the Saskatchewan banner "nationally." The next year Coldwell was elected an MP, as was a young chap from Weyburn who was active in the youth wing of the CCF, Tommy Douglas.

In the 1930s Williams and a dedicated band of grass-roots agrarian socialists laid the organizational foundations for the most successful provincial section of the CCF-NDP. At the heart of this organization, which was to become the envy of politicians across Canada, was an agrarian ideology that saw small producers on family farms as the basic economic unit. Women, men and children all worked together to make the farm productive. Using the same model, they established strong poll and constituency organizations. A man was usually the president, but often the heart of the organization and real leader was the woman secretary. Many of them were capable former rural school teachers who had married local farmers and were the best-educated people in the farm district. Williams deliberately recruited these intelligent, disciplined, well-organized women. Whole families, including the grandparents and the children, would pitch in during an election, working with harvest-time zeal. They "hauled votes" to the polls, just as they hauled their valuable grain, dairy products, or livestock to markets. In the days when there were no big contributors and no income tax deductions for political donations, the party relied on small personal donations and funds from turkey suppers, dances and picnics.

In the 1930s and '40s the CCF placed great emphasis on the political education of the grass-roots people. People read political pamphlets and hundreds of books mailed out from the Wheat Pool Library and the Provincial Library. They shared the party's newspaper and other publications which encouraged debate, such as the Wheat Pool's paper, *The Western Producer.* Study groups met around kitchen tables or in local schoolhouses. During the Depression, Saskatchewan was hit hardest of all the provinces, and most people in the province were near destitution and on some form of relief. More people in Saskatchewan than in any other province suffered from, or died of, tuberculosis, the disease of poverty. With a radicalism born of desperation many lost faith in old ideas and the old-line parties. They were open to any and all new ideas. Whole communities turned out to political meetings to listen to three-hour speeches. If they did not like the speech, some threw ripe tomatoes or rotten eggs. Louise Lucas, along with numerous other CCF speakers, toured the province. She spoke in almost every town, village and city in Saskatchewan and in hundreds of remote, cold, rural schoolhouses lit with coal oil lamps. Coldwell said that she made more speeches than any CCFer in Canada. A plain, pioneer farm woman with a deformed arm, Lucas impressed people as sincere and dedicated. Lucas spoke German in addition to English, a tremendous asset in a province with many Germans. Her one basic speech on the ABCs of socialism helped to convert hundreds of people. She would speak to anyone, anywhere, anytime, in the hope that "the scales would drop from their eyes." One fellow complained, after an exhausting tour of the province with her, that she had "no terminal facilities." She would return to the farm home where she was billeted, "drink a cup of tea to revive like the British in the air raid shelters" and talk into the small hours of the morning. One farmer claimed that his wife was in bed recovering for a week after each Lucas visit.

Elderly grass-roots socialists, when queried about their contributions to the party, often reply, "I talked," knowing the power of personal persuasion. Intellectual socialists, such as Sophia Dixon, Carlyle King, Peter Makaroff and Gertrude Telford offered a more complex analysis than Lucas for sophisticated listeners. The feeling in the CCF in the 1930s and '40s was that of a broad-based people's movement that welcomed all who would work for the cause. Dedicated socialists, most of them converted by dire conditions, threw themselves into political work with missionary fervour, vowing to create "a new world."

In the 1938 provincial election, the CCF elected ten MLAs and then another one in a by-election. The 1940 federal election saw five Saskatchewan CCF MPs elected. To foster a new image in 1941, the CCF defeated George Williams who was, by then, regarded as too radical. Instead it elected as its leader the young, witty, moderate Tommy Douglas whose sunny personality, it was hoped, would appeal more to voters.

With the end of the Second World War in sight and the reform spirit surging, the CCF won a landslide victory in the 1944 provincial election, sweeping forty-seven of fifty-two seats. The Saskatchewan CCF elected Gladys Strum as the first Canadian woman president of a political party. In the 1945 federal election it won in eighteen of the twenty-one constituencies in Saskatchewan. The Saskatchewan CCF was at its electoral peak. With astute popular leaders and hundreds of grass-roots workers, it held power for twenty years. It passed the most progressive legislation in North America, including a government-funded hospitalization plan, and built an excellent civil service.

When John Diefenbaker and the Conservatives swept the prairies in 1958, only one Saskatchewan CCF MP was elected — in the constituency of Elsie Gorius, the best of the CCF organizers. In 1962, '63 and '65, the CCF lost every federal seat in the province. When Diefenbaker put through federal transfer payments sufficient to finance the Medicare program that the CCF had promised ever since the 1930s, the Saskatchewan CCF proposed instituting Medicare. Meanwhile, Tommy Douglas resigned as premier and went "to the East" to head the New Democratic Party. Taking over as premier, Woodrow Lloyd was at the helm when Medicare passed and the doctors went on strike in 1962. The province was polarized as it had never been before when the powerful doctors were backed by the Keep-Our-Doctors Committee and the Liberals under the leadership of Ross Thatcher. The Saskatchewan Medicare scheme, which was to be the pattern for the current federal plan, was the first such plan in North America. The climax of a long campaign for better medical services led by rural women, begun back in the days of the Women Grain Growers, the plan gave free medical services to all. The fee-for-service basis of the program was a shining example of the art of the possible, rather than the state medical scheme with doctors on the payroll envisioned by the radical socialists of the 1930s.

A former CCF MP, Ross Thatcher had crossed the floor of the House to become a Liberal. He learned valuable organizational skills when he was a CCFer from Olive Wells, an outstanding CCF campaign manager, and was able to set about organizing the Liberals very effectively. In 1964 they capitalized on discontent with an old government and the bad feelings aroused during the Medicare crisis to oust the CCF. In spite of Thatcher's rigidity and their virulent anti-socialist propaganda, the Liberals left many of the popular CCF programs in place, while announcing that the province was "open for business."

Out of office for the first time in twenty years, the CCF began to rebuild. Part of this rebuilding was the establishment of a Provincial Women's Committee under the capable leadership of Pemrose Whelan. The PWC planned to fight to get the party back in power, but once organized it was influenced by the modern women's movement and also began to campaign for a more equitable role in the party, which had never had a strong feminist influence. The Saskatchewan CCF women had been dedicated socialists rather than feminists.

Although the federal NDP was launched in 1961, the Saskatchewan CCF did not become the Saskatchewan NDP until 1967. Not merely a change in name, this heralded a significant shift in the party. While the CCF in Saskatchewan had been a rural-based, agrarian, socialist party dominated by farm people, the NDP is an urban-based party dominated by social democrats and trade unionists. Saskatchewan was changing as it urbanized, mining expanded, and agriculture modernized in the post-war period. Large-scale mechanization increased farm size, and the number of farmers declined. With big grain sales to Russia and China, farms prospered, old farmers were able to retire, and the big new farmers were increasingly conservative.

After the 1964 defeat the party moved to the left with the Waffle but, pragmatic as usual, as support for the Liberals began to weaken, the party moved to the centre. It elected Allan Blakeney as its new leader, and aimed at getting back into power. In 1971 the party governed once again, this time with more urban people at the helm. Part of the expanded potash industry was nationalized. In spite of strong opposition from anti-nuclear NDP members, uranium development was encouraged. Human rights legislation was introduced, labour legislation improved, dental and prescription drug programs established and provincial budgets balanced.

In 1982, with neo-conservative, competitive individualism steam-rolling over Britain and North America, the NDP, which idealized co-operation, went down to a dismal defeat at the hands of the Conservatives. The Conservatives had replaced their leader, Dick

Cullver, with Grant Devine, an enthusiastic, young, respectable agricultural economist. Retaining only eight of sixty-four seats, the NDP reeled. There would appear to have been numerous factors leading to the defeat. A streamlined technocratic approach and Blakeney's personal reserve had helped to make the NDP government appear increasingly remote from the people. Many farmers had not liked the administration of the Land Bank program that had been designed to curb corporate and foreign ownership of farmland and to help intergenerational transfer of farmland. Nor did they like the new Marital Property Act, which required an equal division of assets upon the dissolution of a marriage. Both were seen as threatening the traditional patterns of land control by individual male property-owners. On the other hand, in spite of good legislation and changes in party structure, many women were increasingly discouraged with the NDP's dismal record in electing women legislators. There was also a great deal of discontent with the government's handling of Indian land claims. "The Family of Crown Corporations" and the reliable "tried and tested" premier failed to excite an electorate coping with high interest rates and inflation. Unions had gained strength but trade unionists were furious when the NDP broke a CUPE strike and forbade further strikes during the election. Many trade unionists refused to support the NDP.

In 1982, the new Conservative government announced that the province was "open for business" and went into debt to encourage private enterprise, with few results. With patronage rife, they attacked social services, claiming that the welfare state, which the CCF-NDP had established, eroded individual initiative. The federal Conservatives came through with big farm subsidies just prior to the 1986 provincial election so they retained the countryside, which had a disportionately large number of seats, but the NDP won the cities by large margins and won the popular vote. With thirty-eight seats to the NDP's twenty-five, the Conservatives held on to power. Blakeney resigned and Roy Romanow became the new leader.

Declining world markets, drought, its hinterland economy, and government corruption and mismanagement meant that Saskatchewan was in deep trouble. The Conservatives sliced health services, higher education and social programs, and fired civil servants. Premier Devine's respect for the Prime Minister, who is widely despised, and their large increases in taxation added insult to injury. The government launched a large-scale privatization program to sell the Crown corporations and contract out government work to private business. They met more opposition than they expected from a people who still have strong social democratic roots.

In 1991, Saskatchewan appears to have lost patience with neo-conservatism, having had a double federal-provincial dose. Even with a better-educated population than any other province, once again it is caught in the iron grip of a depression. Child poverty is the worst in Canada, people flee in search of jobs, and more aboriginal people commit suicide than in any other area of the world. If elected, the NDP will face the prospect of attempting to revitalize a desolate province. Many of those who hold on are sustained by the enduring Saskatchewan tradition of rebellious practical idealism.

Manitoba

Nelson Wiseman

The social democratic tradition in Manitoba extends
back to the 1880s, when labour organizations appeared
which were committed to improving the lot of their
members and social conditions generally. The dramatic
explosion of Manitoba — expanding from 65 000 to
more than a third of a million people between 1881 and
1916 — coincided with the growth of socialism as an
international movement. That movement, in Canada as
abroad, was critical of the irrationalities of industrial
capitalism and was dedicated to transforming it: to placing
people ahead of profits and socially beneficial production ahead of private gain and ostentatious consumption.
As a new society, Manitoba arose in a more modern age
and offered relatively fertile soil for socialists, unions
and progressive farmers' movements, certainly in com-
parison with the older and more tradition-bound regions
of the Maritimes, Quebec and Ontario.

The earliest exponents of a social democratic outlook
were craft and industrial unionists. The former were
represented by such groups as the International Typographical Union. The printers were highly trained crafts-
men, literate, and organized around their specialized,
technical skills. The industrial unionists were of a more
diverse and generally a more radical type than the craft
unions, built from larger industrial firms. They presented

a noble, dignified, and co-operative vision of society as an alternative to the unregulated, dehumanizing labour market. They lobbied for innovations from monetary reform to income tax and co-operatives, but they also bargained practically on working conditions and wages.

By 1894 a Winnipeg Trades and Labour Council was formed and the following year Manitoba's first version of the Independent Labour Party appeared. Its constitution required that at least three-quarters of the members be wage earners. In 1899, twenty-seven separate unions marched in the May Day parade, and the following year, Winnipeg elected Canada's first Labour MP, Arthur Puttee, editor of *The Voice*, the West's leading labour publication.

In 1913, one immigrant arrived in Canada for every eighteen residents — an influx unparalleled in North America. Many of them headed west immediately: to and through Winnipeg, which mushroomed to become the Dominion's third largest city. Growth was fed by railroad yards second only to Chicago's, and the city acted as the supply centre for the prairies, the bread-basket of the Empire. In 1916, more than half of Winnipeg was foreign-born; there were as many British-born alone as there were native-born Manitobans. Residentially segregated, the city was one of contrasts: the working class, the poor, and the European immigrants lived in the north end; there was a concentration of British workers in the city centre; and a wealthy and generally Ontario-born commercial and industrial élite was ensconced in relatively luxurious quarters on the broad streets and by the rivers in the south end.

Not surprisingly, the social democratic tradition fared best in central and north Winnipeg, where it it took root faster than anywhere else in Canada. Evidence of the direct link between British Labour and Manitoba Labour were the visits of future British prime minister Ramsay MacDonald and Keir Hardie, Labour's founding leader, in 1906 and 1907 respectively. The British party served as a role model and provided the personnel for the emerging Manitoba party. All of the leaders of the Winnipeg General Strike, except for J. S. Woodsworth, emigrated to Winnipeg from Britain between 1896 and 1912, years when there was no real rise in wages in the mother country. Two of these Britons, Fred Dixon and Richard Rigg, were elected as MLAs in 1914 and 1915.

An impediment to further political advance was the left's broad spectrum. A proliferation of labour-socialist parties fed sectarianism. Most of them were moderate parties preaching the municipal ownership of utilities such as gas and water and agitating for the eight-hour work day. Others were more radical; some, like the One Big Union, favoured syndicalism (where workers own and run their industries) and some, like the Social Democratic Party and later the Communist Party, hailed the Russian Revolution and the Bolshevik model. The competing parties included the Canadian Socialist League, the Socialist Party of Manitoba, the Manitoba Labour Party, the Dominion Labour Party, and the Labour Representation Committee.

By 1919 the Canadian labour movement was already a militant force, but nowhere as dramatically evident as in Winnipeg where 25 000 workers — union and non-union, skilled and unskilled — struck for six weeks in an event that brought international attention. In the aftermath of the General Strike, which was concerned with establishing the principle of collective bargaining, arose another reformed Independent Labour Party in 1920, the party whose direct lineal descendants are the CCF and NDP. A political prescription of gradual reform rather than class revolution was preached by social-gospel clergymen such as Woodsworth and William Ivens, who had allied themselves with the union cause and the working poor. The strike's imprisoned leaders became political martyrs; more gravitated to the ILP. John Queen, convicted of seditious conspiracy, was elected from his jail cell to his seat in the legislature. He served seven terms as mayor of Winnipeg in the 1930s and 1940s. Others associated with the strike's cause, including Woodsworth, A. A. Heaps, S. J. Farmer and Marcus Hyman succeeded (or continued, as in the case of Fred Dixon) as elected politicians. In 1912 Woodsworth was elected to the federal Parliament. By 1923 the ILP (also active in Brandon, smaller centres like The Pas, and Winnipeg's suburbs) had elected members to the federal and provincial parliaments and held more than two dozen municipal seats, including the mayoralty of Winnipeg. In 1925 A. A. Heaps became the second ILP member of Parliament in Ottawa.

One faction in the ILP was suspicious of farmers, for they generally opposed the strike; another faction felt that as a narrow labour and city party, the ILP forfeited hope of ever winning power. For most of the 1920s farmers were excluded from ILP membership. Although labour and independent farmer MLAs appeared to co-operate and share common concerns in the early 1920s, their political strategies diverged: the farmers threw their lot in with the Progressives who were absorbed by the Liberals; Labour MLAs held out for a social democratic agenda. Aiding the ILP was the union movement's rejection of the American Gompers philosophy, which precluded direct political involvement.

The birth of the national CCF in 1932 would have been more difficult without the help of Woodsworth and the others. Some ILP leaders, such as Queen, opposed the CCF's formation as a dilution of socialist principles.

He never felt completely comfortable within the new creation until many years later. By the early 1940s, the ILP diehards had faded in influence and the CCF had taken root. Despite efforts to reach out to the rural areas, the party remained a Winnipeg organization, drawing heavily on the turn-of-the-century British immigrant arrivals and their children. In the 1920s, 85 percent of its aldermen were British-born; in the 1930s, 70 percent. It was the same with its MLAs and MPs.

The Second World War was both a challenge to and an opportunity for the CCF. Woodsworth the pacifist opposed Canada's participation in it, but the ILP vociferously urged all-out, concerted, war against fascism. Although British Labour and the national CCF rejected talk of coalition government in London or Ottawa, the Manitoba CCF entered a unique coalition, one featuring Anglo-America's first socialist cabinet minister: CCF leader S. J. Farmer. The coalition was a disaster for the party; it shrank to a record low three MLAs in 1941 but broke with John Bracken's government when he left to lead the renamed Progressive Conservatives two years later. In 1945 the party benefited from its long-standing advocacy of rational, humane and consciously driven public policy planning, a program undertaken during the war but threatened with dismantlement after its end. Rising like a phoenix, the CCF led the popular vote in the 1945 provincial election but ran third in seats on account of its urban concentration in an electoral system with a rural bias.

Throughout the 1930s and 1940s the CCF was alternately courted and condemned by the Communist Party, which behaved as Moscow's faithful ideological lapdog. The Communists called CCFers "social fascists" and other times named them "left adventurers" for opposing Mackenzie King's government. Although the CCF ignored and repudiated Communist overtures, the emergence of the Cold War led some opponents of social democracy to argue that embracing the CCF was tantamount to stepping toward totalitarian communism. The CCF's support plummeted, three of its MLAs were expelled for parroting the Communist line, and the CCF predictions of an impending post-war depression were proven false. The party shrank to fewer than 800 members in the mid-1950s, its lowest point, yet it rebounded in the late 1950s under Lloyd Stinson, who like many CCF-NDP leaders had studied at United College. The CCF briefly held the balance of power in the legislature in 1958–59 and influenced much of the agenda of public policy.

When the CCF was transformed into the NDP at the start of the 1960s, more CCFers opposed the change in Manitoba than anywhere else in Canada. Opponents like Howard Pawley feared, as Queen had in the 1930s, that the new party would water down the older party's socialist heritage. The majority, however, led by Stanley Knowles, prevailed. Where the ILPers had been mistrustful of farmers, the recalcitrant CCFers were suspicious of organized labour. The protests on both occasions came to naught and party transformation, if not revitalization, proceeded. In both cases, fears of a "sell-out" were unwarranted, and allayed: the policies and personnel of the NDP were a continuation of the CCF just as the CCF had been an extension of the ILP. The new CCF did not win over many farmers in the 1930s, and the new NDP did not win over new labour support in the early 1960s. It had that support all along. The NDP fared poorly in its first Manitoba election in 1962, compared to the old CCF in 1959, losing votes in every constituency but one and attracting only 15 percent of the votes.

Two elections later in 1969, however, the NDP won office after a meteoric rise. It came exactly fifty years to the day after the end of the Winnipeg General Strike. Unlike the Conservatives and Liberals, both of whom vacated the centre of the political spectrum in 1968–69, the NDP expanded ideologically and socially to become a centre-left party with its selection of Ed Schreyer as leader. By 1971 a tentative NDP minority government was converted into a confident majority as a result of two by-elections which confirmed that the 1969 election was no fluke. Ethnic interaction, cultural integration, urbanization and a more democratic electoral map all helped catapult the NDP out of its perpetual third-party status into government. The party's early British working class character was transformed and expanded over time to include the ethnic minorities, poorer farmers, and the less privileged. They rallied to the party's banner and especially to its first non-British, non-Protestant leader. Schreyer was the right leader at the right time. Without him the NDP would not have won.

The party was re-elected with increasing support in 1973. Although it lost power in 1977, it was firmly established in the centre rather than on the periphery of provincial politics. In and out of office, the party has championed fairness, social welfare, equality, and compassion in public policy. A flurry of NDP reforms in the 1970s included the elimination of Medicare premiums, revamped labour laws, tax credits for the poor, expanded public housing, public automobile insurance, a reorganized City of Winnipeg and heightened status for natives, women, and the French language.

When the NDP returned to office in 1981, under Howard Pawley, it was the only practical and seasoned alternative to the Conservatives. Evidence of the NDP's unrivalled leadership on the left was the appearance of

Rolland Penner, the son of a long-time Communist alderman, as the Attorney General. By the time it lost power suddenly in 1988, the NDP had become the province's dominant party, having held office for fifteen of the previous nineteen years. After a crushing setback in which it fell back to third-party status, it rebounded in 1990 to form the Official Opposition. It is now well positioned under the leadership of Gary Doer to return to power later in the 1990s.

Although the future in politics is more difficult to foretell than the past is to retell, the NDP seems firmly established as a permanent, long-term, serious contender for office. It now has roots extending well beyond its historical base in Winnipeg, roots that reach into the far-flung native north and the marginal farming and interlake districts. It is neither a passing fancy nor a fringe party as the Progressives and Social Credit proved to be. The story of the Manitoba NDP reveals it has been the most successful provincial wing of the party since the late 1960s. Its policies of the 1970s and 1980s currently serve as models for the fledgling fraternal NDP government in Ontario.

Ontario

Donald C. MacDonald

Electoral success normally requires a combination of effective party organization and a public desire for change. Without effective organization, the desire for change can go unfulfilled; without a public desire for change, a good organization can be ineffective. If there is a near-perfect combination of both, conditions may result in a few candidates being swept into the legislature in spite of having little, or no, local organization. This was the experience of the Ontario NDP in its sensational election of September 6, 1990.

The road to victory had been a fifty-year roller-coaster: from no seats to thirty-four (within four of the Conservative minority government) in 1943; reduced to near oblivion, with only two seats in 1951; struggling back to major party status in 1967; gaining Official Opposition status in 1975, again in 1987, and finally majority government in 1990.

There were many contributors to this successful electoral combination, but as with any social democratic party, the basic element was people, harnessed into an effective team, both within the party and among the supportive groups. These teams were the result of years of patient building.

Originally, there were the pioneers of a host of progressive movements who launched the CCF in 1933, a socialist party with a cohesive philosophy and a goal of something more than incremental reform. During the 1940s, thousands of Ontarians, dissatisfied with the old parties, joined the party and, contrary to the public perception arising from the ebb and flow of electoral fortunes, most of them remained loyal supporters. For example, even when CCF MPPs dropped from thirty-four to eight in 1945, the party's popular vote held in the 400 000 range, but those numbers were swamped by the massive turnout for the Tories in response to the anti-socialist scare tactics of business and propagandists like A. K. Trestrail and Gladstone Murray.

The electoral disaster of 1951 and the doldrums of the 1950s did result in a drop in membership, and popular support languished at around 15 percent. But the Ontario party was revitalized with the re-formation of the ranks of Canadian socialists as the CCF evolved into the New Democratic Party. Political gains were marginal in the first provincial election in 1963, but within a year a resurgence was evident in the Riverdale provincial and Waterloo South federal by-elections, and in 1967 the party tripled its seats.

A larger and more sophisticated team at the party and caucus levels played a critical role, but there was an even more important reason for this breakthrough: in the mid-1960s, NDP membership more than doubled, from 10 000 to 25 000. A people's party cannot be built without thousands of people; for the first time there were enough troops on the ground to begin to cope with the well-organized and well-financed Tories. The result was immediately evident: major party status regained in 1967, Official Opposition in 1975, and missed by only one seat in 1971 and 1977.

However, we must retrace our steps to acknowledge other components of the CCF-NDP team. Heading the list, from the days of the original pioneers, were the organized workers of the trade union movement. They moved through various forms of official support in the early years to sharing in the founding of the New Democratic Party in 1961. The following thirty years saw a persistent educational and organizational effort to persuade individual workers to become party voters and activists. Moreover, during the 1980s, the trade union movement reached out to become a central partner in a growing coalition of community groups, thereby softening, if not eliminating, its false public image of excessive self-interest.

Women have played an important role in the CCF-NDP from its pioneering days, not only in the so-called auxiliary activities, but also in executive positions. Following one convention in the latter CCF years, every executive committee in the Ontario party — including such traditional male reserves as organization and finance — was chaired by a woman. Notwithstanding this relatively favourable record, the effects of socialization and systemic discrimination resulted in great under-representation of women, in the party as in society.

The emergence of modern feminism in the 1960s gave new impetus to the women's movement. Since its goals are an integral part of the socialist program, women became more active in the party. In 1983, the federal party's constitution was amended to require gender parity in convention elections to the council and executive. Since 1983, too, all Ontario party committees have been elected or appointed with equal numbers of men and women.

Among the parties the NDP almost invariably ran the most women candidates. Too often, however, they were nominated in unwinnable seats, but that situation improved significantly during the 1980s. The party's solid commitment, and efforts to fulfil it, were dramatically confirmed in the 1990 victory: nineteen of its seventy-three MPPs are women; nearly half of the first cabinet — eleven of twenty-six — are women; and on the two top cabinet committees, Management Board and the Policy and Priorities Committee, there is gender parity. Full equality for women has yet to be achieved, but with victory and the resulting power, the Ontario NDP has taken a giant step forward.

Two other groups bolstered the NDP team over the years. First was the growing number of new Canadians. As the population assumed a greater cultural mix, especially in Toronto where one-half of Ontario's immigrants settled, the NDP organized an ethnic council in the 1960s, to give voice to the newcomers in the councils of the party. Later, that council was supplemented with "*sezioni*," service centres in the predominantly Italian communities. Still later, a special division of the leader's office co-ordinated the efforts at strengthening ties with the various cultural groups. Traditionally, those political ties had been almost exclusively with the old parties — Liberals federally and Conservatives provincially. Over a generation or more, the NDP gradually established working relationships with the new groups — in the tradition of J. S. Woodsworth with western Canadian immigrants — and they responded with growing representation in caucus and finally in government.

Ontario farmers were the most resistant to the democratic socialist appeal. They have traditionally been a solid core of Ontario's basically conservative population. In the first years of the CCF, the remnants of the United Farmers of Ontario, which had formed the 1919–23 government in coalition with the Independent Labour Party, briefly federated with the party, but soon withdrew in face of what they perceived to be the radicalism of the party and trade unionists.

Interestingly, the NDP won the support of farm leaders before that of the rank-and-file. Nearly fifty farm leaders became members of the Farm Committee at the provincial founding convention in Niagara Falls in 1961. In 1977, Gordon Hill of the Ontario Federation of Agriculture and Walter Miller of the Ontario Farmers Union stood as NDP candidates. At the 1981 election, OFA President Ralph Barrie stated that the NDP program was the best, but that farmers would not be likely to vote for it. Notwithstanding this neutrality, if not hostility, the NDP consistently championed the farmers' interests — notably producer-controlled marketing and income stabilization — even when old-party support wavered. Ironically, after all the years of limited electoral support, it was the votes of rural Ontario in a dozen or more ridings that carried the NDP from the uncertainties of minority to the stability of majority government.

By 1990, the Ontario NDP had built an organization more able to confront the greater resources of the old parties. But was there a compelling desire for change among the public, the other requirement for electoral success? When the election was called, virtually no one felt there was; pundits predicted the Liberals would win more seats. But during the five weeks of the campaign, the desire for change emerged in an astounding fashion, in good part because of the wide-ranging coalition of interest groups who felt that the Liberal government had not been responsive. Through their earlier outreach efforts, the party and the trade union movement had developed a working relationship with these independent groups — environmentalists, anti-poverty coalitions, teachers, nurses, social workers, churches, peace activists and nuclear disarmament advocates — a new breed of political pioneers. Together they created a climate at the grass-roots level which made it possible for a people's party to win.

With such a team it is perhaps not surprising that the NDP victory produced a caucus and a cabinet more representative of the people of Ontario than ever before. The impact of the victory has been felt across the country; overnight party prospects soared, federally as well as in the provinces. Thousands of NDPers, hitherto reconciled to never winning, and a growing proportion of the general public, disillusioned with "old-style" politics but convinced that power could never be wrested from the established parties — all took on new hope. If the NDP could win in wealthy and conservative Ontario, victory is possible anywhere.

Québec

Michael Oliver and Charles Taylor

How do you mix two nations and democratic socialism in a federal state? Nearly thirty years after the NDP was founded, the answers to that question are little clearer than they were at the end of the 1950s. Indeed, the question itself needs to be rephrased to take account of the claims of multiculturalism and the first peoples. Yet when one looks back, the way we defined the principles on which to build a social democratic party that could be as readily accepted in Québec as in other provinces of Canada seems to have stood the test of three decades extraordinarily well. We believed that French Canada must be seen to constitute a nation, and that Canadian federalism must be "asymmetrical," i.e., that Québec could not be considered a province with powers and privileges identical to those of all the other provinces. In the post–Meech Lake era, the chances of preserving Canada still seem to rest on the acceptance of those principles. We can be proud of having enunciated them as party policies at the founding convention in 1961 and at the 1963 federal convention. No other Canadian political party did so then; only now are Liberals and Conservatives edging towards these policies.

To say that the NDP got things right in terms of principle does not win us the right to hide the fact that in organizational and electoral terms the NDP in Québec has yet to be successful. One of the reasons a new party was founded in 1961 was to give the democratic left of Canada a chance to put down roots in Québec that the CCF had never been able to grow. It cannot be denied that the NDP has done better than the CCF ever did; indeed, the federal party led the other parties at the public opinion polls in the 1980s on one or two occasions and, in 1990, it broke the federal electoral barrier and returned Philip Edmonston to the House of Commons in a by-election. To pretend that the expectations of 1961 were fulfilled, however, is futile.

Explaining the failure of the CCF to penetrate Québec is much easier than accounting for the NDP's lack of success. From the CCF's founding in 1933, there was a minimal party organization centred in anglophone Montréal. Minutes of its meetings were kept in English and its pockets of strength were in largely English-language areas like Verdun and the Jewish districts which flanked Park Avenue and St. Lawrence Main. What little money was scraped together to permit a "respectable" list of candidates to run in each federal election and to pay their deposits (which were almost always forfeited) came in great part from the national office of the party. As well as the loyal English Canadians — Dr. J. Cyril (Flynn) Flanagan, Bruce Robinson, Abe Tafler, Bill Dodge and others — there were a few long-term, dedicated franco-phones like Guy-Merrill Desaulniers and Michel Chartrand, and from time to time new recruits to leading roles like Jacques Perault, a professor of law at the Université de Montréal, and — a most exciting addition — Thérèse Casgrain. Nevertheless, the party was all too obviously an emanation of English Canada. Québec had always been in the picture; Montréal socialist thinkers like Frank Scott, J. King Gordon and Eugene Forsey played key roles in the founding and in the continuing evolution of the party. But no French-speaking Quebeckers had been at the core of the CCF back in the formative days of the Regina Manifesto.

A key reason for the failure of the CCF to penetrate francophone Québec had little to do with language and culture. Shortly after the party's founding, the Archbishop of Montréal, Monseigneur Gauthier, issued a warning (*mise en garde*) against Catholics becoming involved with the CCF because of its socialist character. Although this caution, equivalent to a ban in what was still an overwhelmingly Catholic community, was withdrawn in October 1943, it was done in a way that minimized the positive impact it might have had: the Canadian bishops, meeting in Montréal, simply declared that Catholics might support any political party except the Communists and made no special mention of the CCF. The negative position of the church meant not only that popular support for the CCF was difficult to come by, but also that the potential francophone leaders who came forward in Québec prior to 1943 tended to be marginalized in their community by their very willingness to go against clerical injunctions. The New Democratic Party never laboured under such a disadvantage and, ironically, clerical disapproval would have mattered much less in the 1960s than it did in the thirties, forties and fifties.

In Québec, the period just before the founding of the NDP had much to do with the shape that the party finally took. This was the eve of the Quiet Revolution. A rural, traditional culture was giving way to the patterns of thought and values of an urban, industrial society. Trade unions, even the "Catholic syndicates" founded on the basis of corporatist doctrine, were becoming militant under a new, often university-educated, lay leadership. The link between nationalism and conservatism was being broken by the influential editorialists of *Le Devoir*, who could share with the team that published *Cité Libre*, led by Pierre Trudeau and Gérard Pelletier, a set of liberal and often democratic socialist ideas that, in both cases, reflected the personalist doctrines of the French review *Esprit*. The universities, and especially the Social Sciences Faculty of Laval, were replacing the Thomist shibboleths of the philosophy and theology faculties with the economic ideas of Keynes and social and political ideas from Chicago and the London School of Economics. French-language radio and the new television medium provided careers that no longer had to be shaped according to parochial values and permitted men and women like René Lévesque, André Laurendeau and Judith Jasmin to convey a vital, universal as well as local, French culture to wide Québec audiences.

Given the circumstances of Québec in 1960, especially the remarkable victory of the rejuvenated Liberals under Jean Lesage, it was perhaps inevitable that the focus of thought and activity among social democrats in the province was the forthcoming founding convention of the national party. The Québec Committee was bound that the program and constitution of the new party would reflect the Québec of the Quiet Revolution in the most unambiguous fashion; and the Québec members of the National Committee spent much of their time making sure that the reports the National Committee would present to the founding convention would embody the Québec positions.

However, conventions have a dymnamic of their own and the work of planners can be brought to naught by a motion from the floor that suddenly captivates the delegates. The program committee of the founding convention steered through without notable change the policies then of most concern to Québec: co-operative federal-

ism, equality of rights for the French and English lan-
guages, the right of a province to opt out of joint federal-
provincial programs within provincial jurisdiction
without financial penalty, and the recognition of French
Canada as a nation. Within the constitution committee,
however, the euphoria of English Canadian delegates at
the presence and participation of so many francophone
Quebeckers led to substituting "federal" or "Canadian"
for *every* use of the word "national" to describe offices
or functions for the federal party. From the constitution
committee, the spirit of welcome and accommodation
for French Canada spread to the floor, and the bizarre
partnership of Michel Chartrand and Hazen Argue
successfully sponsored a motion which denied the term
"national" to the New Party itself. Finally, the party
elected both a federal president, an associate-president
and a vice-president from Québec, respectively Michael
Oliver, Gérard Picard and Roméo Mathieu. If what was
needed to root the New Democratic Party in Québec was
an acceptance of that province's "distinctness," the
founding convention seemed to have turned the trick.

Perhaps the hoped-for sequel to the founding convention — the establishment of a *Nouveau Parti Démocratique du Québec* — would have occurred smoothly and
effectively had it not been for the intrusion of two
factors.

The first factor that militated against the foundation
of a solid Québec NDP was the necessity for whatever
forces could be rallied, unorganized though they might
be, to fight two successive federal general elections in
1962 and 1963. The election campaigns in Québec had
their moments of glory. In 1962, Charles Taylor attacked
Pearson and the Liberal Party over the decision to allow
nuclear warheads on Canadian-based missiles during a
lively campaign with Pierre Trudeau in Mount Royal;

C.G. Gifford amassed a large vote in Notre Dame de Grâce; and the party's vote on the Island of Montréal amounted to close to the national average for the NDP. Yet the elections revealed just how superficial were the differences in popular response between the old CCF and the new party which had been formed with such high hopes. Trade union support fell far short of expectations, in terms of organizers seconded to party work, of funds and of votes. Real help came largely from unions, formerly affiliated to the CCL, whose national offices had supported the CCF: the United Steelworkers, the United Packinghouse Workers, and the Canadian Brotherhood of Railway, Transport and General Workers. Neither election resulted in a single seat being won in Québec; both absorbed energies and resources that otherwise could have gone into the prompt creation of a Québec party.

The second factor was the rapid rise of Québec nationalism, especially among students, in its *indépendantiste* form. The Québec Liberal Party was being pushed in nationalist directions and it was becoming clear that effective opposition to them would be radical nationalism, rather than either the conservative formulas of the old *Union Nationale* or any kind of left-wing alternative that was not enmeshed with the values of national self-realization. To those who wished to be in the vanguard of social and economic change in the province — those who had come to the NDP because they thought that party was where social democratic action would take place in the new Québec — the lure of a radical Québec nationalism gradually became overpowering.

When finally a first step to founding the party was made at a *Congrès d'Orientation* in 1963, the result was scission along nationalist/federalist lines. By the narrowest of margins, those who supported a separate *Parti Socialiste du Québec* formally dissociated from the NDP but collaborating with it when it wished, won out, and those who persisted in the original intention of forming a Québec *Nouveau Parti Démocratique* parted company with them.

The *Parti Socialiste du Québec* (PSQ) was short lived. In spite of taking with it the only two paid (from the federal office) NDP staff, André L'Heureux and Jean-Claude Lebel, the PSQ was unable to create the organization and raise the funds needed to survive. Somewhat battered, the federally based NDP entered a new phase, with Robert Cliche and Charles Taylor teamed in a strong renewal campaign which finally created the Québec party in 1965.

The 1963 federal convention of the NDP marked the end of the first phase of the party's life in Québec. In policy terms, it consolidated and extended the positions taken with respect to federalism at the founding convention by, first, redefining the party's commitment to a "two nations" concept of Canada and, second, giving precise recognition to Québec's special status by according to that province alone the right to full compensation if it opted out of any federal-provincial joint program.

The next five years saw the second major attempt of the party to implant itself in Québec. A great number of the intellectual and trade union supporters of the New Party period had now left, and had either retired from the fray or thrown in their lot with the PSQ. But very fortunately, the party had made an exceptional new recruit in the 1963 election in the person of Robert Cliche. Cliche came from rural Québec, but was familiar with Montréal. He proved able to put the party's message in a way that got across to Quebeckers to an unprece-

dented degree; indeed, one might say to a degree un-
matched before or since.

Cliche led the party from 1963 to 1968. These were
years of building, largely in new milieux where the party
had not been present before: in some of the small towns
of Québec, for instance, and even in some rural areas.
But it was also a time in which constitutional issues were
coming more and more to the fore. The independentist
movement was building in Québec, not so much in the
party formally committed to sovereignty, the *Ras-
semblement pour l'Indépendance Nationale*, as in a
more diffuse way among trade unionists, teachers, pro-
fessionals, communicators, who were members of other
parties or none. It was the rise of this climate which had
brought about the split with the PSQ.

Even within the ruling Liberal Party, sympathy for
independentism was growing, notably in the circle
around René Lévesque. The NDP was forced to address
this issue again. The solution favoured by Robert Cliche
was that of a special status for Québec within a federal
structure. He remained to the end of his life unconvinced
by the independentist thesis, although he was a close
friend and admirer of Lévesque. Cliche argued within
the councils of the federal NDP for a policy along these
lines.

The notion that a way might be found to accommo-
date Québec without a general redistribution of power
towards all the provinces, thus weakening the central
government, appealed to many people in the party across
the country, and a position paper in favour of a special
status was eventually adopted at the federal convention
of 1967 in Toronto.

On this basic platform the NDP-Q fought the next two
federal elections. In the first of these, in 1965, Cliche
contested his home riding of Beauce. He made a more

than credible showing, but it wasn't possible in that short space of time to overcome the years of resistance towards the CCF-NDP in rural Québec. A decision was made that for the next election, Cliche would run in one of our areas of fastest growth in support, in the new suburbs around Montréal. He chose a riding on Laval Island, and set about building a competent organization.

In fact, we almost made it. In 1968, the year of Trudeaumania, Cliche just narrowly lost Duvernay to Eric Kierans. It is painful to think how the history of the party in Québec might have been different if a leader of Cliche's stature had got a seat in the House of Commons. But the close-run defeat turned out to be a decisive setback. The year 1968 was also the year in which the *Parti Québécois* was founded. Lévesque carried a number of Liberals with him into the new movement, and established independentism as a major option on the Québec scene.

It is significant that the *Parti Québécois* was building towards its foundation in the same period as we were preparing for the election. What was more significant is that both parties were recruiting the same people. Cliche's organization in Duvernay turned into the PQ constituency association a few months later, virtually without change.

With the defeat on the federal level, and the rise of the new option on the provincial level, the entire landscape of Québec politics changed. The potential constituency for social democracy was more and more polarized by the PQ. Not only was there less energy left over for political action at the federal level, but the PQ, quite naturally, considering its option, did its best to discourage support for the NDP. The party had missed perhaps its greatest historic opportunity to break through in Québec. It now had to await better times.

New Brunswick

Richard Wilbur

Central Canadian pundits viewing New Brunswick from afar invariably conclude that here is Canada's most parochial, conservative province, with an aversion for political innovations. A closer look at New Brunswick's history reveals that while the two old political parties have always prevailed, so too has the dissident left. Contrary to conventional wisdom, New Brunswick has always had a reform tradition serving to goad the old-line groups into recognizing the need for change.

The two most important "goads" in the nineteenth and early twentieth centuries were two remarkable native sons, Martin Butler (1858–1915) and Henry Harvey Stuart (1873–1952). One study of Butler in the *Journal of Canadian Fiction* describes him as "the one-armed journalist-newsvendor-poet-socialist-itinerant pedlar-entertainer-temperance-advocate-Canadian National-ist." Although he had almost no formal education, Butler somehow learned to read and write, and after losing an arm in a factory accident he became a pedlar and a poet. In 1890 he began publishing *Butler's Journal*, a monthly which he produced and distributed regularly until his death in 1915. In his stinging editorials, he defended "The Rights of Labour" and extolled the virtues of the honest workers and farmers of New Brunswick. According to Jim Chapman, Butler "abhorred all aristocracy, all privilege, and all exploitation whether by states or capitalists. His editorials contained the foundations of a radical, if vague, reform program which proved attractive to young Stuart."

Although Butler was a Roman Catholic and Stuart a Methodist at a time when such things mattered, they became friends. Stuart, whose Christianity led him to socialism and socialism to the social gospel, in 1902 organized the first socialist party in New Brunswick, the Fredericton Socialist League. He himself was president and Martin Butler, whom he converted to the cause, served as secretary. By the outbreak of the First World War, four other branches had been established at McAdam, Albert, Newcastle and Saint John.

From 1910 to 1919, Stuart was the editor of the Newcastle *Union Advocate*, and his first editorial was entitled "Socialism in Canada." It was through his efforts that J. S. Woodsworth spoke in Newcastle in 1910; and from this grew a friendship that was firmly established long before the birth of the CCF.

While living in Newcastle, Stuart helped spark the rise of a radical element within unionized labour which managed to survive until 1920 when the United Farmers of New Brunswick and the Labourites joined forces to contest the provincial election of that year.

In that historic election, third-party politics flourished among farmers and workers in New Brunswick. The United Farmers of New Brunswick, formed in 1918, was essentially a farmers' co-operative movement but as the 1920 election approached, its leaders established ties with various branches of the Independent Labour Party. In the ensuing contest, the Liberal government was returned with exactly half of the forty-eight seats. The twenty-six UFNB candidates received 21 percent of the vote and nine were elected. In addition, two candidates running on a joint Farmer-Labour ticket were elected in Northumberland County. The latter included the president of a local union composed of lumberworkers and industrial workers. Unfortunately, despite a huge effort by Stuart and a handful of other socialists, the United Farmers quickly moved away from any permanent ties with Labour. After the collapse of Ontario's Farmer–Labour government in 1921, the short-lived marriage of these traditional antagonists broke up. In New Brunswick, the trade unions and the Federation of Labour turned back to industrial action and away from politics.

During these years, two veteran Moncton supporters founded a socialist newspaper, *The Pilot*, while the Saint John local of the Socialist Party of Canada survived to become a charter member of the CCF after its formation in 1933.

On March 1, 1933, at the annual meeting in Fredericton of the New Brunswick Federation of Labour, A. W. Jamieson of the Moncton Trades and Labour Council, noting the desperate state of the local labour force, moved that the NBFL "sponsor and use its machinery to bring into being a branch of the Co-operative Commonwealth Federation in the province of New Brunswick." This surprise resolution carried by a vote of twenty-one to nine after a long discussion, and a call went out to labour, farmer and other groups for a meeting at the Moncton Labour Temple on June 23. About 100 delegates showed up for the historic occasion and voted to sponsor the creation of a New Brunswick branch of the Co-operative Commonwealth Federation. That same day, over a thousand citizens jammed the Moncton Stadium to hear J. S. Woodsworth's keynote address at the founding convention.

Despite the party's early start, it took New Brunswick's CCF organizers eleven years before they decided to enter candidates in a provincial election. This delay was primarily due to the opposition from old-time political forces to new political candidates. In addition, the Moncton Trades and Labour Congress, probably the party's biggest support in the labour movement, failed to persuade the TLC's national convention to affiliate with the new party.

The outbreak of the war ended the unemployment problem and as that conflict neared its final days, it was clear that the CCF star was on the rise, especially after the historic victory of T. C. Douglas in Saskatchewan. This breakthrough in June 1944 probably helped persuade New Brunswick's CCF party to contest forty-one of New Brunswick's forty-two ridings in the election two months later. Its leader, J. A. Mugridge of Saint John, emphasized that the CCF was a "people's party" and dismissed the old-line parties as "monopolists." The Conservatives especially were threatened by the CCF supporters whose organization was strong in the rural, agricultural counties that were traditionally Tory.

The CCF in New Brunswick had good reason for being confident. In July 1944, just a few weeks before the provincial election, it had seventy-five CCF clubs and a month later this climbed to eighty-seven. By November of that year, York County alone had fourteen.

When the votes were tallied from that August 1944 election, the CCF supporters' hopes were dashed: they failed to elect any members.

In 1946, at its annual convention, the New Brunswick CCF passed a resolution "that all Maritime provinces are exploited by Central Canada monopoly capitalism and therefore have organization problems in common." It called for an interprovincial Maritime CCF council. At the inaugural meeting of the Maritime CCF council held in Sackville, Fred Young was named Maritime director of organization.

Despite this new approach and countless rallies and meetings, the CCF could find only twenty candidates for the 1948 general election, and collectively they finished farther down the polls than four years earlier. During the 1949 federal election, York-Sunbury had a unique slate with the president of the University of New Brunswick, Milton Gregg, for the Liberals and a local history student, Murray Young, representing the CCF. Gregg got 12 158 votes to his PC rival's 11 127, while Young got 1628 votes — 500 fewer than his total when he headed the four-member CCF slate competing in the 1948 provincial election. Young later returned to UNB and taught history there until his retirement in 1989.

The CCF's rapid decline in general popularity during the 1950s was especially marked in New Brunswick and Nova Scotia. According to Ian McKay, as the national CCF "came closer and closer to winning mass support, [it] suddenly faced a right-wing propaganda offensive of enormous proportions." Employers warned their workers that jobs could not be guaranteed if the CCF won, and a number of active CCFers were fired. The ultra-conservative press compared the CCF with Hitler and editorials barely hid their antisemitic tones when referring to the efforts of David Lewis, the party's national executive director.

The Edmundston-Madawaska area of northwestern New Brunswick provided a good example of how reform-minded citizens changed their political colours in the face of such pressures. In the 1944 provincial election, Harry Marmen came third in the two-member riding of Madawaska; both he and his CCF running mate lost to the Liberals but finished well ahead of the two Conservatives. In 1948, Marmen ran again, but as an independent. Four years later, he ran as a Liberal but this time three Tories took all the seats in the expanded riding. It is not difficult to imagine the great pressure Marmen experienced from his conservative neighbours (and employers) for declaring his socialist beliefs, and from the old-time parties, notably the Liberals, anxious to capitalize on his obvious popularity.

The transition from CCF to the New Democratic Party that began in 1956 with the Winnipeg Declaration and ended with the birth of the new party in 1961 received mixed reactions from Maritime socialists. New Brunswick, which had been the first province in the region to organize a CCF unit, was the last to shift over to a NDP organization. During most of the 1960s, which produced three provincial elections (1960, 1963 and 1967) the party was dormant. The only time it fielded candidates was in 1967 when three, including the provincial leader, ran in Northumberland.

It was much the same story federally. During the several elections called during the 1960s, New Brunswick's tiny group of NDPers was hard pressed to find token candidates. Repeatedly, it relied on three elements of support:

- committed trade unionists, centred in Moncton, Saint John and Newcastle;
- university staff, mostly at the University of New Brunswick in Fredericton; and
- old CCFers who had been active in the glory days of the 1940s.

The NDP's national office in Ottawa supplied general campaign literature as well as funds to cover candidates' deposit fees. Local supporters always came through to meet expenses for meetings and local advertising. While great efforts were made to draft policy statements specific to the New Brunswick situation, the Liberal government's Program of Equal Opportunity stole much of the NDP initiative and that other party's candidates assumed the reform mantle — at least during the spirited election campaigns.

Another diverting factor during the turbulent 1960s was the anti-establishment mood among young Canadians, especially students. Young Acadians were too engrossed in the traumatic changes in neighbouring Quebec to take up with the anti–Vietnam War protest in the United States and other issues nearer to home that might have led to their alignment with the NDP. As well, a few at the University of New Brunswick seemed to have swallowed a dose of Marxist ideology. Faced with these factors, the handful who kept alive New Brunswick's New Democratic Party deserve great credit for resisting the temptation to disband the organization, weak though it was.

In 1970, J. Albert Richardson, a Miramichi woods contractor and union activist, became provincial leader. Outraged by some NDPers who had demonstrated against the War Measures Act, he showed that he was on the right of the party. Given the tumultuous events that had heralded the decade's beginning, it was only a matter of time before Richardson's conservatism would be challenged. About a dozen NDP supporters in the Fredericton area formed what they termed a provincial Waffle group, led by Patrick Callaghan, who had learned his radicalism growing up in Glasgow. They wanted nationalization of most of the economy without compensation, an end to compulsory education and the legalization of marijuana. At a party convention in Saint John, their motions carried the day and Callaghan emerged as the new provincial leader. The right wing of the party persuaded the National Council to declare the convention unconstitutional and a later gathering in Chatham restored the former party leadership.

Predictably, this inner struggle was gleefully exploited by the Irvings, owners of the main English-language media outlets, but despite this embarrassing rift, the party found candidates for most of the English-speaking constituencies in the 1974 provincial election. Under a new leader, former teacher and environmentalist John LaBossiere of Rexton, Kent County, the NDP in New Brunswick gained wide popular support and respect for its stand against the Lepreau nuclear station and the massive aerial spraying against the spruce budworm.

At the same time, the party established links with leaders of the *Parti Acadien*, which had sprung up in the Bathurst area during the early 1970s. While its youthful supporters dreamed of an autonomous Acadian province, the PA leader, Euclid Chiasson, a former philosophy teacher at Collège de Bathurst, shared the NDP's goals for more state-imposed economic and environmental controls. In the 1974 election, the two parties agreed not to run competing candidates in some French ridings, where the Parti Acadien felt it had a chance. This was continued to a lesser extent four years later, and in Kent Centre, John LaBossiere, listed on the ballot as a union organizer, finished a strong second.

Unfortunately for party unity, LaBossiere's public stand against Lepreau and aerial spraying, while it gained many new supporters, antagonized some of his labour colleagues. They feared that such tactics placed too many jobs in jeopardy. Convinced that he lacked a sufficiently broad base to continue, LaBossiere resigned in 1980 and was succeeded by George Little, a Scottish-born high school teacher.

A witty and gifted speaker, Little inherited some key organizational components plus several experienced campaigners. During the 1982 campaign, he stood head and shoulders above the two other party leaders when they participated in a widely viewed television debate. In subsequent public appearances, his verbal skills and broad knowledge of the issues earned George Little and the NDP increasing respect even among some of New Brunswick's most conservative-minded citizens. In 1982, Robert Hall, who had come close for the NDP in the 1978 election, led the polls in the new riding of Tantramar (created in 1974 when New Brunswick created single-member constituencies). The presence of Hall, a highly respected teacher, in the staid old legislature was the best proof that the NDP had come of age in New Brunswick. Even though he would be swept aside in the total Liberal landslide of 1987, Hall's performance won him the respect from the front ranks of the two old parties.

A closer look at the results of that 1987 election reveals the real gains made by the NDP candidates during the four years since the previous contest. In twenty-two ridings the NDP increased its vote, and in urban areas like Moncton and Saint John the jump was substantial, despite the Liberal sweep. This showing reflected the renewed organizational efforts made possible by a full-time staff.

NDP prospects increased even more after Elizabeth Weir became party leader in the spring of 1988. A lawyer, she had been chosen the party's full-time provincial secretary back in 1983. Bolstered by her extensive experience as the party's executive director as well as her legal training and media skills, Weir became the legislature's most formidable critic. Her revelations of Liberal patronage, her initiative in placing environmental issues under public scrutiny and her scathing criticisms of the McKenna government for protecting big forestry companies while doing little to diminish mounting child poverty made her a force to be reckoned with. Despite her not having a seat on the floor of the House, by her superb use of an improvised Question Period and her access to public accounts hearings, Weir frequently was referred to by impressed though frustrated cabinet ministers as "the Leader of the Opposition."

In the general election held on September 23, 1991, Elizabeth Weir made history by becoming the first NDP leader to win a seat in the legislature.

With a full-time executive director, Roger Couvrette, with active organizations and an expanding membership throughout the province, and with a dynamic leader, the New Democratic Party is clearly on the march. For proof positive, look at how New Brunswick's "small-c" conservative voters responded in the December 1990 by-election in Beauséjour. As one journalist put it, "the New Democratic Party gave Jean Chrétien a political black eye to take back with him to Ottawa.... In a riding where they had rarely exceeded 10 percent of the vote, NDP candidate Guy Courmier won nearly 40 percent of the ballots cast and struck deeply into the heart of a traditional Liberal stronghold."

Is this a harbinger of things to come? Before dismissing such thoughts, remember that this is a party whose early supporters founded the New Brunswick Teachers Association, that helped establish New Brunswick's environmental movement, and that has kept alive the tender shoots of democracy enmeshed in a one-party legislature.

Nova Scotia

G. Gerald Harrop

Nova Scotia has not been a hothouse of radical politics.
But in contrast with her sister Maritime provinces, there
has always been a very visible "third force" thrust. In
Cape Breton, for example, throughout the early years of
the twentieth century, the union activities of miners and
steelworkers often resulted in strikes, always bitter, and
sometimes bloody, while in Antigonish the co-operative
movement was another manifestation of an economic
alternative to "branch-office capitalism."

The early story of the CCF-NDP movement and party
in Nova Scotia is concentrated in Cape Breton, although
the first legal trade union in Canada, the Provincial
Workingmen's Association, was founded across the
strait in Springhill in 1879. This was but six years after
such institutions were legalized in Canada. As the in-
tense, sometimes bloody, struggle of the miners for
social justice continued, the PWA was perceived as a
"sweetheart" union. In February 1919, after a bitter and
prolonged contest, J. B. MacLachlan, the legendary
leader of the miners, led his people into affiliation with
the United Mineworkers of America (UMWA) and the
Cape Breton community became District 26 of the
UMWA.

Before the establishment of the provincial Co-operative Commonwealth Federation in 1939, the left made

an impressive, but short-lived, breakthrough in the provincial election of 1920, with a farmer-labour coalition polling 30 percent of the popular vote and electing eleven members. The 1920 result in Nova Scotia reflected the movement across Canada toward rural radicalism. The United Farmers of Ontario were in power provincially from 1919 to 1923. In Alberta the UFA ruled from 1921 to 1935 and in Manitoba the UFM formed the government from 1922 to 1928. In the federal election of 1921 the Progressive Party (rural and western) won sixty-four seats, fourteen more than the Tories. It is unclear why this movement manifested itself in Nova Scotia but not elsewhere east of Ontario.

But this marriage of the rural and industrial did not last long. In the the election of 1925 the rural voter reverted to his traditional habits and the labour candidates were badly beaten, only two holding their deposits. An Independent Labour Party nucleus continued to exist in the early thirties although it was unable to mount an effective political challenge. In the federal election of 1935 it appeared that some future CCF stalwarts, including Donald MacDonald, future president of the CLC, and Clarence Gillis supported the Reconstruction Party of Tory maverick H. H. Stevens. In the summer of 1936, J. B. MacLachlan and some of his friends founded a club in Glace Bay to plan a new political party which would espouse the cause of the miners and other workers. Subsequently this led to the formation of the Cape Breton Labour Party (CBLP). In the provincial election of June 22, 1937, the CBLP contested the Cape Breton East seat, which really meant the town of Glace Bay. The candidate, nominated only ten days before the election, was a United Church minister, the Reverend W. T. Mercer, who polled a very respectable 3400 votes, 32 percent of the total.

In 1938, District 26 of the UMWA sought affiliation with the CCF. At the Trades and Labour Congress Convention in Niagara Falls, several Nova Scotian UMWA leaders met with David Lewis, then national secretary of the CCF. This was the first formal affiliation of organized labour with a political party in Canada. The arrangement was concluded in 1939.

After the UMWA-CCF alliance, the party organized on a provincial level. J. S. Woodsworth attended as the main speaker at the first provincial convention at Sydney in May 1939. Before the arrival of Woodsworth, David Lewis and Angus MacInnis toured Nova Scotia, endeavouring to organize CCF clubs on the mainland as well as in Cape Breton. Clarence Gillis that same year was nominated for the federal seat of Cape Breton South. Lewis and MacInnis left the province with a feeling of happy optimism. Early election results tended to justify the conviction that there was growing support in Nova Scotia for the CCF. On December 5, 1939, the CCF had won the first election it contested in Nova Scotia. Although the CCF candidate, Douglas Macdonald, had not been nominated for a by-election in Cape Breton Centre until twelve days before the election, he won the seat with a five-hundred-vote plurality. Clarence Gillis captured the federal riding of Cape Breton South in 1940.

In the provincial general election of 1941 the CCF succeeded in three constituencies out of the five that they contested in Cape Breton. The year 1945 was a less favourable year; only two candidates were successful. Russell Cunningham carried Cape Breton East and Michael ("Mickey") MacDonald triumphed in Cape Breton Centre in an election where the Tories were effectively wiped out, so that Cunningham became the leader of the Offical Opposition to Angus L. MacDonald's Liberal government. An outcome of the shifting electoral pattern was the increased margin of Clarie Gillis's support in the federal election, which securely established him as the labour spokesman in Parliament, not only for Cape Breton and Nova Scotia, but for the whole country east of Manitoba. Gillis won four successive elections until defeated by a Tory in the first Diefenbaker win of 1957. Although Gillis was no longer on the scene, he left behind a legacy which enabled NDP candidates to twice win his old constituency of Cape Breton South.

After the Second World War the national leaders of the party, led by the secretary, David Lewis, persuaded the provincial executive to move party headquarters from Glace Bay to Halifax. The doctrine was that in every province across the country provincial CCF headquarters should be in the capital city. This move was deeply resented by Cape Bretoners. After all, the party's strength and electoral successes had been concentrated in their area. Throughout its history the party has had to cope with this Cape Breton–mainland dichotomy. In Cape Breton, the CCF was basically a labour party, its leaders being union officials. Its emphasis in policy was on "bread and butter" issues. Mainlanders were often regarded as "pipe-smoking" theorists who looked upon politics as a continual seminar, pondering the nature of the free and just society while those in Cape Breton manned the barricades. Many people believed that as a result of the transfer of party headquarters its standing fell to only one elected member, Mickey MacDonald in Cape Breton Centre in 1956. MacDonald kept his seat until his defeat in 1963. The popular vote across the province had shrunk from 13.6 percent in 1945 to 4.1 percent in 1963. The year 1967 was another difficult year for the party: no members were elected. These years became the low point in party fortunes.

With the election as party leader of Jeremy Akerman, a Cape Breton school teacher, the party strength in Cape Breton recovered. Akerman and Paul MacEwan were elected in 1970, both on the island, although the total popular vote across the province rose to only 6.6 percent. In 1974 a third member was elected and the total vote rose to 13 percent. A fourth member joined the group in 1978 and the vote increased once more, to 14.4 percent.

Paul MacEwan described this period in his book, *The Akerman Years*, in which he contrasted the revival of the seventies with the quiescent sixties and blamed that decade's decline on the Halifax intellectuals, including party leader Professor Jim Aitchison. The Akerman era ended with the expulsion of MacEwan from the party for failure to co-operate with its constitutionally elected leaders (some of whom he called "Trotskyites") and also for alleged fund mismanagement. About this time Akerman stepped down, accepting a high-profile and well-remunerated civil service position in the Tory government of John Buchanan.

The year 1980 saw Nova Scotia New Democrats elect a woman, Alexa McDonough, a Halifax social worker, as leader. McDonough had run a creditable campaign in the federal constituency of Halifax in the 1979 election, and in 1981 she won the provincial seat of Halifax Chebucto. This was our only victory in that election, significant in that it was our first ever victory, provincial or federal, on the mainland. But in that election our Cape Breton seats were lost. Subsequently, good candidates have come close in Cape Breton Centre, but we have yet to regain an island seat.

McDonough was joined in 1984 by her fellow candidates John Holm of Sackville and Bob Levy in Kings South. However, four years later when new elections were called, party morale was severely shaken when

Levy announced that he had accepted a judicial appointment from the Buchanan government. Only McDonough and Holm survived the 1988 election and, indeed, McDonough won very narrowly in Chebucto.

Defections, as well as the continued isolation of Cape Breton progressives, have been the main problems of Nova Scotia New Democrats. The party gained in popular vote during McDonough's leadership, going from 15.9 percent in 1984 to 16 percent in 1988. However, the high point had been reached still earlier, with 18 percent in 1981.

The recent experience of the Ontario NDP, which grew in support until it achieved majority government, gives us hope. In a true three-party system one must receive at least 30 percent of the popular vote to be a contender for government. This must be our present aim in Nova Scotia. The scandals surrounding the Buchanan régime in 1990 were climaxed by the deeply cynical Senate appointment of John Buchanan while still under RCMP investigation for corruption. The revelation that the Liberal leader's salary had been augmented by a secret party fund, has, we hope, opened for us a door of opportunity. But there is much work to be done before we can take advantage of Buchanan's amoral behaviour. The polls show increasing respect for our leader and for the party. Our membership is growing, as is our financial support. Alexa McDonough is becoming established as a potential leader of the government as her dedication, honesty and intelligence are recognized.

Although Nova Scotia has not been a province where the two traditional parties have been seriously threatened, there has been a steady, and sometimes effective, third force on the left. This is seen in union militancy, especially in Cape Breton, and in the "Antigonish" co-operative movement. There have been times of electoral success for democratic socialism, especially in Cape Breton. And since the election of McDonough as leader in 1980, there has been a good increase in the popular vote on the mainland, especially in Halifax-Dartmouth. This has unfortunately been off-set by defections and distrust of "mainlanders" in Cape Breton. This division seems now to be healing and Nova Scotian New Democrats look to the future with guarded optimism.

Since its founding in 1939, the CCF-NDP in Nova Scotia has kept alive in a conservative community the vision of a truly free and just society.

Prince Edward Island

Douglas MacFarlane

The first Co-operative Commonwealth Federation organization in Prince Edward Island was set up in the Bedeque area on a June evening in 1936, under the direction of E. J. "Ted" Garland, who was visiting the province on behalf of the national CCF organization. Local leadership was spearheaded by Rev. Arthur Organ, then pastor of Bedeque United Church. Reverend Organ had been leader of a study group during the preceding winter. Part of the material studied was the book, *Social Planning for Canada*, written by a group who might have been considered the "brain trust" of the CCF.

At a meeting in Central Bedeque Hall, study-group members debated the subject of capitalism versus socialism. Then Mr. Garland gave a comprehensive talk on the CCF. Following the meeting, a party club was organized. Charter members included W. N. Jenkins, Irving Toombs, Hector Leard and Douglas MacFarlane.

The original CCF club held a few meetings, but its activities eventually petered out. However, enough interest remained to make the area a focal point for further activity.

In 1939, the province was visited again by an organizer from the national CCF, Dr. J. Stanley Allen, then a member of the faculty of Sir George Williams College,

Montreal. He visited the Bedeque area where a house meeting was held. He also explored whether interest in the CCF existed elsewhere in the province. No great results, but the flickering flame of party interest was kept burning.

Early in 1943, the national CCF decided to take further measures to stir up activity in the province. A national CCF council meeting was soon to be held and arrangements were made to cover the costs of an Island delegate. Douglas MacFarlane attended that meeting. During the next few months, he visited various centres in the province that had shown interest in developing a CCF organization.

The year 1943 was a provincial election year. The CCF supporters were ready. A surprising interest was shown in the Wellington area, where Cyrus F. Gallant and Napoleon Arsenault ran in the 3rd Prince riding. Six other candidates rounded out the CCF list. We did our best to make our presence felt in the province.

Until 1943, joint political meetings had been the tradition during election campaigns. However, in the 1943 election, the old-party candidates refused to face the CCF and the party lost the publicity value these meetings would have provided. Nevertheless, the party now qualified for CBC "Provincial Affairs" radio time, and we made good use of it. That same year a provincial convention was held, with a fine speech given by Joe Noseworthy, MP for South York, who had defeated Conservative leadership hopeful Arthur Meighen in a by-election in 1942. Irving Toombs was elected president and Douglas MacFarlane was chosen provincial secretary.

The party contested all four seats in the 1945 federal election. During the election campaign the party had its first full-time organizer in the province, Ken Green, a native of Albany. We were making progress.

A provincial by-election was held in the 5th Prince (Summerside) electoral district in December 1945. Douglas MacFarlane was asked by some Summerside people to run for the CCF. This turned into a real contest — when it otherwise might have been an acclamation. This gave the province's Liberal government an excuse to raise candidates' deposits from the traditional ten dollars to fifty dollars. This might sound trivial, but it was enough to deter many candidates. However, it didn't deter the party from fighting sixteen seats in the 1947 provincial election, winning a substantially increased vote from 1943. The re-elected Liberals then raised candidates' deposits further to two hundred dollars.

The 1951 provincial election was called when the spring roads were almost impassable. This, plus the high candidates' deposits, meant the CCF was able to run only five candidates. However, one of the candidates in the 4th Prince, J. Harrison MacFarlane, brightened the picture by carrying his own poll. Running such a small slate, however, meant that the party lost its CBC "Provincial Affairs" radio time. More difficulty came when the position of Maritime organizer was terminated.

The CCF contested no more provincial elections, but had candidates in the 1953, 1957 and 1958 federal elections.

Prince Edward Island helped pioneer the candidature of women with Hilda Ramsay and Muriel MacInnis, who participated in the provincial and federal election campaigns of 1951 and 1957 respectively.

When the time came to build a new, more broadly based movement, the plan for the New Democratic Party was endorsed by the Island. It sent a sizable delegation to the founding convention held in Ottawa in 1961. In

November of that year, at a convention in Charlottetown, the Prince Edward Island section of the NDP was established. Ian Webster became provincial president and Lorne Perry vice-president. A public meeting addressed by the new federal leader, Tommy Douglas, drew a crowd of four hundred. In spite of our initial enthusiasm, in the 1962 federal election we only received 5.2 percent of the province's vote. This was not encouraging but we were in no mood to give up. We realized that a long struggle to obtain the confidence of the electorate lay ahead.

The 1963 federal election came entirely too soon to suit the Island NDP. Much of the earlier enthusiasm was gone. However, we fielded a full slate of candidates — and have done so in every federal election since.

Beginning with the 1968 federal election, the province was divided into four single-member ridings. Charlottetown teacher David Hall, running in Hillsborough, made the best showing for the NDP. Subsequently, he became the party's first provincial leader. A little later, however, he decided to leave the province, and the party was leaderless again.

NDP fortunes improved in the 1972 federal election. The party received 8.9 percent of the province-wide vote. Its Cardigan candidate, the popular St. Peter's school principal Aquinas Ryan, made a vigorous campaign pay off with 14.2 percent of the vote. On November 25, at a special leadership convention, he became the party's new provincial leader.

The 1974 provincial election saw twenty provincial candidates enter the field. The party criticized various aspects of the Island's Comprehensive Development Plan. It called for public ownership of public utilities and automobile insurance, and an end to the many forms of patronage. The vote received by the NDP indicated progress, and our members were encouraged by Aquinas Ryan who received 14.6 percent of the popular vote in his constituency. Unfortunately, internal discord within the party resulted in Ryan's resignation. Doreen Sark assumed the leadership temporarily, to head the five-candidate slate in the 1979 election.

A policy review and leadership convention was called for March 13 and 14, 1981. With no leadership candidate in sight, this was an act of faith. However, a new leader, Doug Murray, unexpectedly assumed the role. As a former party organizer he set about his new duties in ambitious fashion; he was especially interested in political education. But his political work was a spare-time undertaking and he couldn't give it the attention he felt it needed. After a year of leadership an old congenital heart condition forced him to relinquish the post.

The annual party convention of 1983 elected Jim Mayne, who had been president of the National Farmers Union, as leader of the NDP. Mayne did a good job of leading the party in the 1986 and 1989 provincial elections. The party's most spectacular electoral achievements came in two by-elections. On December 2, 1985, in 4th Prince, Mayne received 24 percent of the vote and saved his deposit — a first for the party. On September 14, 1987, he came second in 5th Prince, once again saving his deposit and beating his PC opponent.

After the 1989 election, and after much dedicated work and personal sacrifice, Mayne relinquished the party leadership. Dolores Crane, who received the largest vote ever for an Island candidate in the 1988 federal election, became the party spokesperson, pending a leadership convention.

The story of the CCF-NDP in Prince Edward Island is not one of great success, but neither is it one of failure.

We have endured and we intend to remain a force for better and more democratic government. This is our fifty-fifth year of life.

Some of the policies set out in our 1943 and 1947 election programs — the abolition of political patronage, for instance — have not been carried out. But there has been progress with others. The property vote is gone, the voting age is eighteen, education is greatly improved, and so is health care. We have been a constant force for the good, constantly prodding the government to improve the lot of all Islanders.

The party would have accomplished more and would have had greater impact on Island affairs if more people who were involved in our movement had remained active longer. This turnover in party membership often meant we were just holding our own instead of building up strength. As our prospects improve, let us hope that the NDP supporters, old and new, will continue to work long and faithfully together for the common cause. We will endure. And one day our small but faithful force will grow strong and lead the Islanders in a government that will reflect the finest traditions of our small province.

We shall endeavour to bring a better future for Islanders and for Canadians.

Newfoundland and Labrador

Gerry Panting

The decade of the 1960s, in Newfoundland and Labrador, was not unlike that era in the rest of Canada. New ideas were in the air and there was a sense of optimism about the economy and our society. We moved in to the 1970s with great expectations which, in terms of growth and development, appeared to be justified. It was not until the 1980s that we began to experience some doubts and uncertainties.

It was against this changing economic and social background that the New Democratic Party in this province came to birth and growth. Of course, during the 1950s, there were some faint stirrings of a social democratic outlook. However, the Liberals of Joey Smallwood were accepted as a populist party that was going to establish economic growth and a welfare state.

In 1959, a clash between the Smallwood government and the International Woodworkers of America touched off a strike among loggers in the woods industry. One result was the formation of the Newfoundland Democratic Party by a group of newspaper employees and labour people in Corner Brook. They were led by Ed Finn, Jr. He and Calvin Normore were put forward as candidates for provincial districts in the election of 1959. While they did not carry the seats, they made a good showing, which enabled their party to continue in being until the Newfoundland New Democratic Party was organized after the 1961 federal convention.

The leadership of the NDP and the bulk of its membership remained for a time on the west coast of the island and in central Newfoundland because of the strength of unionized labour in these areas. By 1962 and 1963, the Progressive Conservative opposition had begun to gather support. In the 1962 provincial election, the NDP candidate in Corner Brook, Ed Finn, Jr., was supported by the Progressive Conservatives who agreed not to divide the anti-Smallwood vote by running a candidate. He was not successful. On the other hand, the Conservatives were able to elect seven candidates, four of them from outside the Avalon Peninsula. This electoral co-operation did not continue. In the federal election of 1963, the Liberals captured all seven Newfoundland seats. Provincially, in 1966 the Conservatives were reduced to three seats in the east end of St. John's.

At the same time, there was some contact between the NDP activists on the west and north coasts of the island and faculty members of Memorial University and other people in St. John's. For a time, the leadership was undertaken by university people — Fred Binding, a psychologist, was president. In the 1960s, attempts were made to field candidates in both provincial and federal elections. In one of the latter, the party nominated Mary Summers of St. John's. However, the NDP failed to obtain representation at either level of government.

As with the NDP in the rest of Canada, there was a problem in acquiring a following among those who have been recently called "average Canadians." Voters proved to be few and far between in our case. So, those people who were active in the party had to find ways to get the party name into the public eye and consciousness.

In order to do this, it was necessary to provide some kind of continuing organization in the form of an executive committee linked to as many activists as could be identified and encouraged to work in the various areas of Newfoundland and Labrador. From the 1960s down to the 1990s, this has been one of the major tasks for the Newfoundland and Labrador party.

Suffering from the lack of a continuing group of experienced personnel who could carry on the activities of the party, we suffered as well from a lack of continuous records and a lack of funding. Certainly, the succession of strong federal leaders were an inspiration which kept people going despite our disappointing electoral showing. We persisted in our attempts to operate as a political party. At the same time, we were sustained by our ultimate objective of establishing a social democratic society. By the late 1960s, there began to emerge the opinion, constantly expressed in our meetings, that one of our functions was to keep that goal alive until the voters caught the vision as well. So, along with practical economic and social issues, the NDP could be relied upon to put forward the general criticisms of a basically competitive society and a market economy. From this characteristic came the labels "crackpots" and "idealists."

The federal election of 1968 marked a shift in the politics of the province, as the PCs took six of seven seats. In a 1969 provincial by-election our candidate was able to garner about 10 percent of the vote in the district of St. John's East. The Conservatives had held it since Confederation and they won handily. This demonstration of Conservative strength in St. John's continued across the 1970s. In 1971, after a tied election between the Liberal government and the rising Progressive Conservative opposition, the latter, led by Frank Moores, took control of the provincial government. Another election in 1972 provided the Conservatives with a majority government.

The New Demopcrats, as is often the problem with third parties, were caught in the squeeze. The desire to end Liberal rule definitely meant that there were few NDP votes to be garnered. The change in the political balance between the old parties left us at the bottom. Once again, it was back to the drawing board for the party faithful. School teacher John Connors from Grand Falls took on the job of leader at this point. The federal party was prepared to help with the daunting task. But it was difficult to know where to start. Some encouragement was gained from the showing of the party candidate in the federal district of Grand Falls–White Bay–Labrador in 1972. It appeared that the NDP message was getting through.

One event which opened the way to a more promising future was the passage of the Federal Election Act of 1974. This made it possible for those who made donations to the party to get income tax rebates for the amount given. An agreement between the federal and provincial parties made it possible to begin to fund the provincial party from this source. At the same time, "transfer payments" from the federal party for administrative purposes added stability to our provincial organization.

The provincial election of 1975 revealed what appeared to be a new trend in the support for the NDP. While the party fielded only seventeen candidates among the fifty-two seats in the province, the trend in voting in St. John's was of considerable interest. In the capital city's ridings our candidates obtained about 19 percent of the vote, on average. This was important because the proportion of seats allotted to St. John's had risen. In addition, the best returns were not from the centre of the city but from the middle-income suburbs. Therefore, while the 1970s were a decade that saw the strengthening of St. John's support for the new Conservative government, they were to be an era of strengthening NDP support as well. This became evident in the results of a federal by-election in St. John's West where Tom Mayo came in a good second against Conservative John Crosbie in 1976. The riding included rural as well as urban populations. In the following year, the new provincial leader, John Greene, failed by only forty-three votes to capture the completely urban provincial district of St. John's West.

By the end of the 1970s, the rising tide of the NDP in Newfoundland and Labrador was illustrated once again in the federal sphere when Fonse Faour became our first MP from the province. In a by-election following the appointment of Jack Marshall, MP from Humber–St. George's–St. Barbe, to the Senate, the NDP vote rose from 4 percent in 1974 to about 40 percent in 1978. In the following year, our party reached a new high. With a fine slate of candidates, the party was able to retake Faour's seat and register several seconds in other ridings. In terms of the popular vote, the NDP was tied with the Progressive Conservatives at 30 percent.

However, this high point was followed by a devastating slump in support. A provincial election, called immediately after the federal contest by the new Conservative premier, Brian Peckford, ended with the NDP garnering only about 9 percent of the vote. This was a traumatic shock to the party faithful. The gloom deepened when, in 1980, we lost the seat held by Fonse Faour. After his short period as leader, Faour was replaced by Peter Fenwick, who had been a candidate in both provincial and federal elections. He was unable to win the provincial seat of Bellevue in a 1981 by-election.

Although during the 1980s there were to be both provincial victories and another federal victory, this series of setbacks led to a pause in organizational activity.

Peter was able to capture the provincial district of Menihek in the mining area of western Labrador, and retain it in the provincial general election of 1985. As the first provincial NDP spokesperson in the House of Assembly, Peter was a source of rising morale for the whole party. He was joined by Gene Long, who also won a by-election. So the party's provincial profile was raised notably. It appeared that we were on the way to official status as a provincial party. Not only that, but another federal by-election provided the party with its second MP. In 1987 Jack Harris was elected in St. John's East. Unfortunately, despite an improved showing in the subsequent federal general election of 1988, Jack was defeated by the current member, Ross Reid.

In the latest provincial election (1989), Peter Fenwick was unable to run and Gene Long was narrowly defeated. However, in 1990, after the party's victory in Ontario, Jack Harris carried the St. John's East provincial district. Therefore, it now appears that the party is within an ace of becoming an established part of the political scene in Newfoundland and Labrador. As this goes to press, our current leader, Cle Newhook, is fighting a by-election in Trinity North on the east coast of the island.

Part III
The Future

Toward a New Democracy for Canadians

Audrey McLaughlin

On the face of it, New Democrats have a good deal in common with other political parties. We field candidates in elections, faring well in some and less well in others. We campaign hard, we put our views forward forcefully, we fight for what we believe in.

That, however, is where the similarities end. There is a fundamental difference between us and the other parties. It begins with our approach to issues and policies, an approach that carries a different set of values and asks new kinds of questions, culminating in a whole new kind of answer.

It's an approach that puts people before profit, communities before corporations and the needs of tomorrow's children before the power of today's vested interests. Most of all, it's an approach that values the experiences, opinions, and contributions of all Canadians. It is an approach to politics that holds the potential for a new democracy for Canadians.

Addressing economic, political, and social injustices must be the first priority of government. This means that federal governments must work to ensure that every Canadian who wants to work should be able to have a job. Recessions should not allow governments to simply give up on over a million unemployed Canadians. There is a better way.

We must not only "announce" that equality for all Canadians exists, we must also ensure that it happens. This means affirmative action for aboriginal people, women, the disabled and other Canadians for whom the Canadian economy has created so much inequality and unfairness.

If we are to accomplish these goals, we can no longer make decisions behind closed doors. This simply leads to confrontation and creates a climate of winners and losers. If we turned toward co-operation, inclusion and consensus, there would not only be public support for federal government decisions, but the public would ensure that different issues are tackled. The environment would be given the priority it needs, and federal governments would focus on providing jobs for Canadians, instead of tax breaks for the wealthy.

At the root of our values is the fundamental belief in the rights of all humans and in the unique contribution each of us has to offer to our local, national and international communities.

In short, we are interested in a new democracy. A new democracy that is present in both the political and economic spheres of our society.

Today, there are national uncertainties about the values we share as Canadians. I believe this is a result of the failure of successive federal governments and national institutions to reflect and articulate what Canada is all about. Rather than listening to and representing the views and values of Canadians, we see a tendency to promote the views and values of only the corporate élite.

As a result, our federal government seldom hears and rarely listens to the majority of Canadians. Aboriginal people, women, the disabled, the poor, ethnic Canadians, small businesspeople, working families and those of us concerned about the environment are left out. This means that the values they share — the values we share — co-operation, fairness, family, equality, openness, inclusion — are largely ignored in the corridors of power in Ottawa.

Instead, the values of large corporate Canada — profit, greed, survival of the fittest — are the guiding principles of the two old parties which have governed this country. From these values emerged policies like the Canada–U.S. trade deal, cuts to social programs, cuts to funding for women, aboriginal, and minority groups, destruction of our environment and national cultural institutions, the GST, and corporate tax loopholes.

Yet, running a country like a large corporation does not leave much room for a nation's soul. Canada is much more than a marketplace. Surely, the values we share as a nation encompass more than the "the bottom line."

We need a national government and national institutions that truly reflect the values and aspirations of Canadians. I reject the old belief that Canada can be designed from above, that a vision should be imposed by an élite. I believe that Canada can only survive and flourish by bringing together the visions of all Canadians from all communities. If the political system truly reflected Canada, our diversity would be celebrated and our various experiences as groups in a vast nation would be shared.

I entered politics because this is the kind of Canada I believe in: where everyone is involved in the political system, where people have control over the decisions affecting their lives. Imagine a House of Commons that mirrors the Canadian population — where women, aboriginal people, minority Canadians, the poor and middle class were represented in relation to their proportion of the population. Imagine what a different kind of place Parliament would be, how different the priorities would be, and how different the decisions coming out of it would be. Imagine a government protecting the environment, instead of corporate polluters.

Part of the problem is that our political intitutions are designed in a way that works against the values of Canadians. As it stands now, Parliament encourages conflict at the expense of co-operation, the Senate encourages patronage at the expense of accountability, and executive federalism encourages élite decision-making at the expense of democratic participation. Reforms are urgently needed.

Parliament is not the only national institution which needs renewal. Our social programs must be strengthened to ensure equality for Canadians wherever they live. Our transportation and communication networks should better link Canadians from every corner of the country. Our cultural institutions must have the resources and support necessary to celebrate our diversity, and remind us who we are and what we share.

Our goals of true democracy, equality and social justice must also include the international community. Our social democratic vision encompasses all of humanity, reminds us that we are all sisters and brothers, and recognizes that we all have a responsibility to care for each other.

George Bush, Brian Mulroney and others have spoken about the "new world order," which has as its point of departure the Persian Gulf War. What a horrifying thought: that a new era begins by repeating the same mistakes of the past, where the same old destructive way of resolving conflicts is seen as the only answer.

Like millions of Canadians and citizens around the world, I reject that kind of a new world order. I embrace, instead, a vision of a new world community founded on common security, where the security of one nation can no longer be seen as dependent on the insecurity of another. We must learn to emphasize co-operation over confrontation, negotiation over threat, disarmament over arms sales, and collective international action based on protecting peace rather than waging war.

This is a critical time for the world. We must embrace new values that move us forward to peace instead of backwards to war.

This is also a critical time for Canada. We can grow as a nation or we can fail. In order to grow, we must replace the old values of greed, adversarial games, and the egotism of power for power's sake with the exciting and dynamic values of compassion, co-operation, diversity and equality. Together, I believe Canadians can make it happen.

People Come First

Shirley Carr

There are many reasons for supporting a political party.
The most important reasons for me were my family's
background and my personal experience as a case
worker. My family's history goes back to the mines of
Cape Breton where some of them were employed and
where the CCF was the acknowledged representative of
the working people. Although my parents eventually
moved to Ontario, they never forgot their origins. Cape
Breton was a special place where the way of life was
distinct from the rest of Canada, the people hard-working and unsophisticated. My parents were very much
part of this life and from them I would like to think I
inherited many of the values which are precious to me.

My experience in the Social Services Department in
the old Township of Stamford and the City of Niagara
Falls, which later became the Regional Municipality of
Niagara, convinced me that I had to support the New
Democrats. In my roles both as a welfare worker and as
a union leader, I observed life as it really existed for most
Canadians. These experiences have made me acutely
aware of our need to create a satisfactory standard of
living for all of us, without the constant fear of chronic
unemployment — which is so disastrous to the workforce. In the early sixties, the maximum welfare allowance was $180 and to be eligible for it you had to

have a family of eight. The pernicious effect of poverty was not something I had become aware of from textbooks, but rather something I observed daily in my work.

The New Democrats seemed the only political alternative to the old parties. I believed they would understand the ravages of unemployment and the avarice of the marketplace. The other parties did not appear to care. My conviction did not stem from their economic policy alone but rather because for me people come first. Jobs will always be more important to me than high interest rates or policies which deliberately use unemployment as an instrument of government planning. Those who pioneered the New Democratic Party and many of those who followed had as a basis of their political philosophy a decent living for every Canadian. That is also my goal.

As a result of my interest in the New Democrats, and although I was extremely busy in both my local union and the Ontario division of CUPE, I agreed to stand as a candidate for the Ontario election of 1971. I did not win, but we increased the vote substantially. I am proud we finally won the seat in 1990 with Margaret Harrington.

There are some individuals whose example has helped me chart my life course and whom I admire very much. Agnes Macphail's personally autographed picture hangs on my office wall. She was a person whose courage, statesmanship and character influenced me considerably. Her photograph is a constant reminder of her long personal struggle to improve the standard of living for Canadians.

Tommy Douglas was another person whose influence has been important in my life. The inspired manner in which he addressed an audience, his capacity to move people deeply was impressive. I was one of those people whom he moved. Sophie and David Lewis were also marvellous individuals who worked tirelessly for the party and the labour movement. The 1974 convention of the Canadian Labour Congress was memorable, not only because I was elected as an officer but also for David Lewis's outstanding speech condemning wage controls. Stanley Knowles was another who lived his life according to his principles. Such people are rare in any society.

We would like to think that the NDP distinguishes itself by its commitment to principle. From the beginning, the support for human rights around the world has been the backbone of much of their policy. Concern for our own native people and our minorities flowed naturally from this position.

I am very pleased that the NDP has never wavered in its support of labour. We have our differences and will continue to have them. But our aims in the long term are the same. We want a workable partnership. The NDP has shown that they can govern a province and are capable of governing a nation. You do not have to be a lawyer to be a cabinet minister. Perhaps we even have too many lawyers in government, and that may not be good for any nation.

Some critics say that labour should not be involved in politics. Indeed, the National Citizens' Coalition has even taken us to court to stop our support, not only of the NDP, but also of social issues in general. Fortunately, the Supreme Court in the Lavigne case agreed that unions had the right to spend dues on social causes. Indeed, we believe our efforts in support of the NDP have helped improve the lives of Canadians. Whether it is health or child care, unemployment benefits or jobs, we have seen tangible results from the efforts of the New Democrats and the assistance we have given them.

The tragedy that has befallen our country and its people under the Tory-corporate agenda in the last decade demands action. It is our intention to build upon the foundation set by our predecessors — a foundation that has been undermined by free trade, privatization and deregulation.

One day New Democrats will govern Canada. And when we do, it will be done with ability and fairness towards all segments of society, as has happened in other social democratic countries around the world.

My final thought is for the business community. The NDP have always provided honest leadership for the nation and governed well. A New Democratic government will make decisions not to the exclusion of business, but to the inclusion of labour in an orderly society where all of us can work together in harmony.

Social Democracy and Canada's Future

Edward Broadbent

Social Democracy and Canada's Future is an edited version of the last speech given by Edward Broadbent as leader of the federal council of the New Democratic Party in Toronto on March 4, 1989.

As we approach the twenty-first century, I am optimistic about the future of the New Democratic Party and the future of Canada. We all know that Canada as a multi-cultural nation has already accomplished much. Our vast and vibrant country provides richly diverse opportunities for our citizens, new and old alike.

Since the Second World War, we have made great strides: in material well-being and social policy; in painting and writing; in music, sports and movies. We have joined the family of creative, self-confident nations. We see all around us the potential to become an even more exciting and decent society.

We believe that a commitment to economic prosperity is essential, but that this must go hand in hand with a commitment to liberty, equality and community. We believe it is political power that must be used to ensure that these values can prevail in a society with a market economy.

The Market Economy
and the Conservative Agenda

As we close the twentieth century, the serious debate about the future, here in Canada and abroad, is not about the desirability of a market economy. For most thoughtful people that debate is now closed. Market economies have been responsible for the production of more goods and services since the Second World War than were produced in all of previous human history.

The debate in Soviet bloc countries and China is now very much about establishing both democracy and some kind of market mechanism. In the West it is about how existing democratic power should be used. The dividing lines are increasingly clear.

The Canadian conservative economic agenda has been that of Margaret Thatcher and Ronald Reagan.

This conservatism asserts that the best role for government in the economy is no role. According to this ideology, decisions made in the private sector should not only dictate what prices and commodities should be, but should also have the predominant influence in what the priorities of society as a whole should be.

It was concisely put by Michael Wilson when he said, "My budget calls for all Canadians, *not* government to choose what is best for Canada," as if government were not a key instrument of a democratic people. The implication is clear. This abandonment of the role of government to the complete supremacy of the market was also revealed in the Conservative propaganda for free trade. The public good was equated with the corporate good.

Consider that after six years of so-called economic recovery, the national unemployment rate remains higher today than before the onset of the 1981 recession.

Now we have another recession in 1991 from which recovery might be very slow.

Equally ominous are that the gap between the lowest- and highest-paid workers has increased and that incomes of senior executives increased ten times as fast as the incomes of ordinary people. In fact, when inflation is considered, hourly paid workers have actually had a loss in income during the Mulroney years.

Five million Canadians, or perhaps more, live below the poverty line. The human results of these statistics are profound. Feelings of regional unfairness worsen as Newfoundland fishermen and prairie farmers compare their fate with more prosperous parts of the nation.

A record number of Canadian children go to school without breakfast. It is unconscionable to us that while a minority basks in considerable comfort, increasing numbers of Canadians struggle for basic dignity. It is unconscionable that in many parts of Canada our hospitals and our schools should be in decline. It is unconscionable that, going into the twenty-first century, millions of Canadians should be living in poverty. It need not be; it must not be. It would not be with a New Democratic Party government. Neither the Conservatives nor the business community points out that Canada's spending on social programs is already thirteenth out of nineteen industrialized countries, and not changing.

From the beginning of the debate on the trade deal, I said that Canadian social programs and our regional development programs were threatened. Brian Mulroney denied this. I said big business would pressure the federal government more than ever to cut back our programs to "harmonize" them with the United States. While vigorously denying what I said, Canadian business mounted an aggressive advertising campaign in

favour of the trade deal and in support of the Conservatives. An example of what occurred was the way the U.S.
government imposed an enormous countervailing duty
on Sydney Steel rails because they received government
assistance. The business community says nothing while
Canada's ability to remedy regional inequalities is being
taken away and yet they don't hesitate to call for budget
cutbacks in badly needed social programs.

The truth is that corporations engulfed in merger
mania don't give serious consideration to the future of
Canadian communities and Canadian workers. And the
truth is that this Conservative government's philosophy
of the market means they won't include in the coming
budget the required changes to our competition legislation. That's what we need; that's what we should get.

Critical too is the central question of national control
of our economy — Americans already own about 36
percent of our industry. While some U.S. congressmen
are now talking about the need for tougher U.S. laws on
foreign ownership when only 4 percent of their economy
is foreign owned (and they are supported by 80 percent
of Americans), our Conservatives move in the opposite
direction. Even before the implementation of his trade
deal, Mulroney had already dismantled all but a pretence
of foreign investment review in Canada.

The Swedes, the Japanese, the French — virtually
every successful industrial nation — make a distinction
between trade on the one hand and foreign ownership on
the other. When foreign ownership is permitted in sec-
tors in these countries, stringent national performance
and regulatory criteria make sure that their national
interest is met.

The Market Economy and Social Democracy

I believe that Canadians as a whole and not just an élite must be able to make decisions to control our destiny.

The fundamental point I want to make is this: it's only by having social democratic policies by the state representing the priorities of the majority that the values of community and equality can flourish within a market society. Social democrats and conservatives both understand this. The difference is that we believe the power of government should be used to this end, the conservatives do not. Conservatives in Canada, Britain and the U.S. are producing economic growth, but it is accompanied by high levels of unemployment, increases in corporate concentration, growth of regional tensions, and cuts in social programs. Meanwhile, the wealthy obtain a greater and greater share of what is produced.

This need not be the case. While Canada has exhibited all these features under Mulroney, during the same period Sweden, with a government equally committed to a market economy but also politically committed to social democracy, ensured that state power in lawmaking and regulation worked for the common good.

The comparisons with Canada are vivid. Instead of unemployment today over 10 percent, Sweden's is at 2 percent. Earnings are up by 5 percent for Swedish families while real wages for Canadian workers are down. Instead of reducing social programs they have expanded them in Sweden. And instead of toothless environmental legislation, a tough policy of shifting away from nuclear energy has been put in place.

We New Democrats believe in the marketplace. We support private investment decisions, reduced tariffs, private property, the free disposal of assets, the right to make a profit and decentralized decision-making. But we also believe in an activist industrial policy that includes foreign ownership regulations, fair corporate taxes, health and safety regulations, farm marketing boards, making the impact on the environment part of all economic decisions, honest government contracts, worker participation and a worked-out policy goal of achieving full employment. We also believe that certain aspects of social organization, among them health services, should be taken right out of the market.

New Democrats are not content with managing the future. Like Brandt and Palme and Bruntland, we would use the authority of a democratic government to create greater fairness. We would have growth, but we would not simply manage the future, we would create a different future.

The importance of the environment and the urgency of disarmament are good examples. We inherited one of the planet's most beautiful countries. To travel from Newfoundland to Vancouver Island, from Whitehorse to Quebec City in any of the four seasons is a wondrous joy. For too long, we have ravaged Canada's beauty and threatened the heritage of future generations.

As the Bruntland Commission has documented, as television has revealed, as every schoolchild now knows, from the forests of Brazil to the ozone layer protecting the planet itself the problem of the environment is a global one. The human future is conditional upon the appropriate international political action. Henceforth in Canada, the protection of our land, our air, our water and our trees must be non-negotiable.

While millions starve in the Third World, while human priorities are ignored in the industrial world, over a trillion dollars are still being spent annually on armaments. Now is the time to seize the moment and move decisively towards a more stable peace with deeper cuts in armaments of all kinds. Now is the time to ground our national security on a policy of common security. Surely we must understand that if Gorbachev and what he stands for fails, we will see a return of the Cold War and all that means for domestic and international policies in the U.S.S.R.

Canada has acted in the past. Lester Pearson incurred the wrath of Lyndon Johnson on Vietnam, Pierre Trudeau's disarmament moves annoyed Ronald Reagan. They didn't do what they did to provoke the Americans, they did it because they believed it was essential for peace and disarmament.

The Role of the New Democratic Party

As part of the global social democratic movement, our party (CCF-NDP) came into being because of the ravages of the economic system in the 1930s. There was a moral insistence upon the values of liberty, equality and community. There was an insistence that the economic system should be changed to adjust to these human requirements. Rather than force people to adjust to the economy's needs, social democrats say the economy must be forced to meet human needs. Political power is crucial to this end.

Having good moral arguments is one thing, but changing the world is another. The moral obligation of the politician is to use power to improve the human condition. But first he or she must have power. Our predecessors would never have been called "the conscience of Parliament" had they not been elected to Parliament in the first place.

All my predecessors from J. S. Woodsworth to David Lewis understood this. We have pensions and unemployment insurance today because Mackenzie King needed J. S. Woodsworth's and A. A. Heaps's votes in 1926 when they held the balance of power. It was their persistent struggle that finally made these reforms law.

We have Medicare nationwide today because Tommy Douglas and Woodrow Lloyd defeated the business and political establishment of their day in Saskatchewan and showed it could be done.

We have Petro-Canada today because on behalf of the NDP in December 1973, as caucus chairman, I told a Liberal cabinet minister his minority government would come down that week unless he made a commitment to a publicly owned petroleum company. We got the commitment.

Social democratic politics involves both principles and power. To argue only for principles is to be narcissistically self-indulgent. To pursue only power is to deny our reason for being.

It is very rare that a clear-cut choice between principle and expediency must be made. But when the choice has to be made, New Democrats must opt for principle.

In the four years leading up to the 1988 election, the NDP caucus gained an unprecedented level of public support. It did so by vigorously defending what we represented. It did so by pursuing power and by maintaining principle.

When the vote came on capital punishment, we voted no.

Not long before the 1988 election, Canadians responded to a public poll asking them their opinion of eight NDP policies. Because of the work done by the NDP caucus on the environment, on women, on taxes, on regional development, on disarmament, work that combined the pursuit of power with commitment to principle, a majority of Canadians supported a majority of those policies.

I look forward to the day — and it will come in my lifetime — when a New Democrat government in Ottawa will make those policies into law.

While it is true that our social democratic principles are inviolate, this is not true of the policies proposed for their practical application. We do not have a recipe book uninfluenced by time and circumstance that will provide a perfect answer for all of Canada's problems. We must work hard to apply our philosophy to a nation and world that refuses to stand still. As the world evolves so must our policies.

Canada and Quebec

We New Democrats were the first federal party to assert that the uniqueness of the province of Quebec must be constitutionally recognized in a modern Canada. We did so at our founding convention in 1961. For this we were soon castigated by our political opponents. However, after a few years, the other federal parties have seen the usefulness of transforming the inevitable into the desirable. With few exceptions, Canada's political leaders at all levels now see the reality of Quebec as the one jurisdiction in North America that requires corresponding constitutional recognition. This uniqueness of Quebec should be seen as a special jewel within the crown of our constitution.

Economic Democracy

We know that the old Foreign Investment Review Agency was inadequate in the first place. But with the onset of the trade deal and the increasing number of mergers, it is essential that we quickly develop a comprehensive, new industrial policy that can be put before

Parliament. Among other matters to be dealt with is the issue of Crown corporations. In many ways, Air Canada and Petro-Canada have performed admirably. Surely it is time as a party that we face the fact that it is not enough that such public enterprises should function well in the marketplace. Among other things they ought to become models for the future in industrial relations. There is political freedom and industrial freedom. Participation is the key to both. Together with the men and women in the trade union movement, we ought to be developing specific proposals to enhance the decision-making role of men and women in their places of work.

Equality for Women

When I became leader in 1975, only 37 percent of Canadian women worked outside the home. Today almost 75 percent of women of child-bearing age are in the labour force; today there are two million children whose parents work outside the home. Parliament must respond to their needs now.

We have led the way in promoting adequate, affordable child care for all Canadians as a right. Our leadership role must be sustained until full equality between the sexes has been established, until the day arrives that a young boy and young girl, on the same street anywhere in Canada, have equal opportunities to be what they will to be. That has been our goal. It will remain our goal.

Perhaps you will permit me to close with a metaphor, a risky business in political life.

The most distinguished conservative theorist in this century portrayed political life as a voyage at sea. Michael Oakeshott said that politics is essentially a conservative activity. The politician, he stressed, is like the captain of a ship caught in rough seas. According to Oakeshott, his democratic task is simply and exclusively to keep the ship afloat. His task is to listen to people, to resolve conflicts and to keep the peace.

This view of politics contains an important but partial truth. For a social democrat, it is inadequate. It is true that the ship must be kept afloat. But if this is all there is to political life in a secular age it is a view that is at once bleak and unjust.

For social democrats there is a port and there must be charts. We listen but we must also lead.

A model society combining liberty, equality and community is the goal. And although we must listen, and although we occasionally confuse the charts we use with the final destination, charts are nonetheless essential. When certain charts prove to be inadequate or wrong they must be discarded. But the goal remains inviolate.

If civil society is to be anything other than the clash of competing vanities, our goal must be to aspire to a nobler vision and then do what we can to achieve it.

Forsaking neither reason nor passion, indeed obligated to both, our task is not merely to listen but to lead, not simply to manage but to change. Utopia, realizable or not, must be our guide. Democratic political power for the common good must be our means.

Contributors

Pierre Berton
Pierre Berton is the author of thirty-six books, including his latest bestseller, *The Great Depression*, which deals with the formation of the CCF. Many people consider Pierre Berton Canada's unofficial historian.

Edward Broadbent
Ed Broadbent is a former professor of economics and political science. He led the New Democratic Party from 1975 until 1989 when he retired and became head of the Centre for International Human Rights and Democratic Development.

Shirley Carr
Shirley Carr is the first woman president of the Canadian Labour Congress. Her job is to represent Canadian labour and knit together the union movement. It is a task that requires great energy, tact, and mediation. Shirley Carr is now serving her second term as president.

Alvin Finkel
Alvin Finkel is professor of history at Athabasca University. He is the author of *Business and Social Reform in the Thirties: The Social Credit Phenomenon in Alberta* and a co-author of a forthcoming Canadian history survey. He has published a variety of articles on the evolution of the welfare state in Canada, on Alberta political and labour history, and on Canadian immigration policy.

Max Fraser
Max Fraser was editor of the *Whitehorse Star*. Since 1978 he has worked for the New Democrats in every

Yukon territorial and federal campaign. Now he is associated with Tony Penikett, the Yukon premier.

G. Gerald ("Gerry") Harrop

Gerald Harrop has been a supporter and member of the CCF-NDP from the beginning of the movement and party. He was professor of Hebrew and Old Testament Studies, McMaster University and McMaster Divinity College (1950–1978). He is the author of *Advocate of Compassion: Stanley Knowles in the Political Process* and *Clarie: Clarence Gillis, M.P., 1940–1957*. Dr. Harrop has been retired since 1978 and lives in Blandford, Nova Scotia.

David Heaps

David Heaps was parliamentary secretary to M. J. Coldwell from 1945 to 1947. He served in the Canadian Army during the Second World War as an enlisted man and officer, and was awarded the Military Cross. During subsequent years, he has worked abroad for public service organizations concerned with the problems of social and economic development. He has headed development programs in Africa for the Ford Foundation and has worked for various international organizations abroad. He has taught at Yale University and has written articles on contemporary issues for the *Washington Post*, the *New York Times*, the *Christian Science Monitor*, and other papers and journals. He now lives in Princeton, New Jersey.

Leo Heaps

Leo Heaps is the author of twelve books, as well as stage plays and numerous articles. He has been closely associated with the social democratic movement for many years.

Cooper Langford
Cooper Langford is a journalist who has worked for several publications in the Northwest Territories and the Arctic. He now lives in Edmonton where he continues to follow northern affairs.

Alexander B. Macdonald
Alexander Macdonald is former Attorney General of British Columbia. Presently he is a university professor.

Donald C. MacDonald
Donald C. MacDonald was leader of the CCF and the New Democratic Party in Ontario from 1953 to 1970. He was a member of the provincial Parliament from 1955 to 1982, when he relinquished his seat to Bob Rae, the present Premier.

Douglas MacFarlane
Douglas MacFarlane has been dairy farming in Prince Edward Island on a property that has been in his family since 1799. He has for more than half a century been the eyes and ears of the social democrats in that province. He has helped to keep the flame burning on an island where it takes special courage to be a devoted New Democrat.

Lynn McDonald
Lynn McDonald is a professor of sociology and department chair at the University of Guelph. She has been the member of Parliament for Broadview-Greenwood, sitting from 1982 to 1988, and published a book on the NDP, *The Party that Changed Canada*, in 1987. She is a former president of the National Action Committee on the Status of Women.

Audrey McLaughlin
Audrey McLaughlin is a member of Parliament for the Yukon. She is the first woman to head a political party in Canada. As leader of the New Democrats, she follows in the footsteps of Ed Broadbent and faces some formidable challenges in a turbulent Canadian era.

Kenneth McNaught
Kenneth McNaught has written numerous books on the political history of Canada. He is recognized as one of the nation's outstanding scholars in his field.

Michael Oliver
Michael Oliver was the first federal president of the New Democratic Party. He has been professor of political science at McGill University, director of research for the Royal Commission on Bilingualism and Biculturalism, and president of Carleton University. He returned to Canada recently from four years in Papua New Guinea. Michael Oliver served as a soldier in World War II and was in the fighting lines in numerous major campaigns, where he distinguished himself for his bravery.

Gerry Panting
Gerry Panting is a former leader and secretary of the provincial New Democratic Party of Newfoundland and Labrador and is the party's current president. He is also a professor of history at Memorial University.

Tony Penikett
Tony Penikett is Premier of the Yukon Territory. He was first elected to the Yukon Assembly in 1978 and served as president of the federal New Democratic Party from 1981 to 1985.

Charles Taylor
Charles Taylor is professor of philosophy and political science at McGill; author of a recent book on the modern identity, *Sources of the Self;* was vice-president of the federal NDP during the late 1960s and early 1970s; ran four times in Québec, and was a close collaborator of Robert Cliche when he led the Québec party.

Georgina M. Taylor
Georgina M. Taylor is a Carleton doctoral candidate and a lecturer at the University of Saskatchewan. A member of the Saskatoon Women's Calendar Collective which wrote the 1980 and 1981 *Herstory,* she has had several articles published. She did an oral history project and a master's thesis on Saskatchewan CCF women. She is now doing research on Violet McNaughton's agrarian feminism.

Larry Wagg
Larry Wagg has devoted himself to the trade union movement since early adulthood. He is a printer.

Alan Whitehorn
Alan Whitehorn was researcher for David Lewis's memoirs, *The Good Fight*. He is currently at work on a book on the CCF-NDP and is a professor of political science at the Royal Military College in Kingston.

Richard Wilbur
Since 1957, Richard Wilbur has been teaching Canadian history and commenting on regional issues. An expert on the 1930s, Wilbur's latest work is *The Rise of French New Brunswick*. Since 1988, he has been supervising the research service of the New Brunswick Legislative Library.

Nelson Wiseman
Nelson Wiseman currently teaches political science at
the University of Toronto. He has also taught at York
University and the University of Manitoba and is the
author of *Social Democracy in Manitoba: A History of
the CCF-NDP*. He has published several scholarly articles on prairie politics, Quebec, and voting behaviour.

Suggestions for Further Reading

J. S. Woodsworth

MacInnis, Grace. *J. S. Woodsworth: A Man to Remember.* Toronto: Macmillan Co. of Canada, 1953.

McNaught, Kenneth. *A Prophet in Politics: A Biography of J. S. Woodsworth.* Toronto: University of Toronto Press, 1991.

Mills, Allen. *Fool for Christ: The Political Thought of J. S. Woodsworth.* Toronto: University of Toronto Press, 1991.

A. A. Heaps

Heaps, Leo. *The Rebel in the House: The Life and Times of A. A. Heaps, M.P.* Markham: Fitzhenry & Whiteside, 1984.

M. J. Coldwell

Bird, John. *Leading Personalities of the CCF Convention.* Ottawa, 1948.

Coldwell, M. J. *Left Turn Canada.* London: V. Gollancz, 1945.

Tommy Douglas

McLeod, Thomas H. and McLeod, Ian. *Tommy Douglas: The Road to Jerusalem.* Edmonton: Hurtig Publishers, 1987

Shackleton, Doris French. *Tommy Douglas.* Halifax: Goodread Biographies-Formac, 1983.

Grace MacInnis

No biographies of Grace MacInnis have been published.

Agnes Macphail

Crowley, Terry. *Agnes Macphail and the Politics of Equality.* Toronto: James Lorimer & Company, Publishers, 1990.

Pennington, Doris. *Agnes Macphail: Reformer.* Toronto: Simon and Pierre, 1989.

Stewart, Margaret and French, Doris. *Ask No Quarter.* Toronto: Longmans, Green, 1959.

Stanley Knowles

Harrop, Gerry. *Advocate of Compassion: Stanley Knowles in the Political Process.* Hantsport: Lancelot, 1984.

Trofimenkoff, Susan Mann. *Stanley Knowles: The Man from Winnipeg North Centre.* Halifax: Goodread Biographies-Formac, 1986.

David Lewis

Lewis, David. *The Good Fight.* Toronto: Macmillan, 1981.

———— *Louder Voices: The Corporate Welfare Bums.* Toronto: James Lewis & Samuel, 1972.

———— and Scott, F. *Make This Your Canada.* Toronto: Central Canada Publishers, 1943.

Smith, C. *Unfinished Journey.* Toronto: Summerhill Press, 1989.

The Federal NDP

McCormack, A. R. *Reformers, Rebels and Revolutionaries: The Western Canadian Radical Movement.* Toronto: University of Toronto Press, 1977.

Morton, Desmond. *The New Democrats, 1961–86: The Politics of Change.* Toronto: Copp Clark Pitman, 1986.

Young, Walter. *The Anatomy of a Party: The National CCF, 1932–61*. Toronto: University of Toronto Press, 1969.

The Yukon

Johnson, Linda R. *With the People Who Live Here: A History of the Yukon Council, 1909–1961*. Draft manuscript in preparation for the clerk of the Yukon Legislative Assembly.

Morrison, David R. *The Politics of the Yukon Territory, 1989–1909*. Toronto: University of Toronto Press, 1968.

Turner, Arthur J. *Somewhere a Perfect Place*. Vancouver: The Boad Foundation, 1981. 69–77.

The Northwest Territories

No studies of the party in the Northwest Territories have been published.

British Columbia

Robin, Martin. *The Rush for Spoils, 1871–1933*. Toronto: McCelland & Stewart, 1972.

———. *Pillars of Profit, 1934–1972*. Toronto: McClelland & Stewart, 1973.

Young, Walter D. *The Origin of the CCF in British Columbia*. The Ormsby B.C. Studies. Vancouver: The University of British Columbia, 1976.

Alberta

Finkel, Alvin. *The Social Credit Phenomenon in Alberta*. Toronto: University of Toronto Press, 1989.

Mardiros, Anthony. *William Irvine: The Life of a Prairie Radical*. Toronto: James Lorimer & Company, Publishers, 1979.

Saskatchewan

Archer, John H. *Saskatchewan: A History.* Saskatoon: Western Producer Prairie Books, 1980.

Biggs, Lesley, and Stobble, Mark, eds. *Devine Rule in Saskatchewan: A Decade of Hope and Hardship.* Saskatoon: Fifth House Publishers, 1991.

Greunding, Dennis. *Promises to Keep: A Political Biography of Allan Blakeney.* Saskatoon: Western Producer Prairie Books, 1990.

Manitoba

Smith, Doug. *Let Us Rise! An Illustrated History of the Manitoba Labour Movement.* Vancouver: New Star Books, 1985.

Stinson, Lloyd. *Political Warriors: Recollections of a Social Democrat.* Winnipeg: Queenston House Publishing, 1975.

Wiseman, Nelson. *Social Democracy in Manitoba: A History of the CCF–NDP.* Winnipeg: University of Manitoba Press, 1985.

Ontario

MacDonald, Donald C. *The Happy Warrior: Political Memoirs.* Markham: Fitzhenry and Whiteside, 1988.

Morton, Desmond. *The New Democrats, 1961–86: The Politics of Change.* Toronto: Copp Clark Pitman, 1986.

Québec

Lamoureux, André. *Le NDP et le Québec, 1958–1985.* Montréal: Editions du Parc, 1985.

Sherwood, David H. "The NDP and French Canada, 1961–1965." Diss. McGill University, 1966.

New Brunswick

Chapman, James K."Henry Harvey Stuart (1973–1952): New Brunswick Reformer." *Acadiensis* Spring 1976.

Garland, Robert. "Promises, Promises...An Almanac of New Brunswick Elections, 1870–1980." *Social Sciences Monograph Series,* Special Issue 1 (1979).

McKay, Ian. "The Maritime CCF: Reflections on a Tradition." *New Maritimes* July-August 1984.

Nova Scotia

MacEwan, P. *Miners and Steelworkers.* Toronto: Samuel Stevens Hakkert & Co., 1976.

MacLean, T. "The CCF in Nova Scotia, 1938–5." *More Essays in Cape Breton History.* Ed. R. J. Morgan. Hantsport: Lancelot Press, 1977.

P.E.I.

Smitheram, Verner, Milne, David, and Dasgupta, Satadal, eds. *The Garden Transformed: Eleven Critical Essays on Modern Prince Edward Island.* Charlottetown: Ragweed Press, 1982.

Newfoundland

No studies of the party in Newfoundland have been published.